Heloise's work
and money savers

Heloise's work and money savers

by Heloise Cruse

PRENTICE-HALL, INC. Englewood Cliffs, N. J.

*I dedicate this book with all my heart
and soul to every housewife and
homemaker . . . all of whom are overworked*

Other books by Heloise Cruse
HELOISE'S HOUSEKEEPING HINTS
HELOISE'S KITCHEN HINTS
HELOISE ALL AROUND THE HOUSE

Heloise's work
and money savers

Introduction

We all have days when we get disgusted, but have patience, these too shall pass . . .

So now that you have this book in your hand, pull up a good rocking chair.

All settled?

The first thing you must learn is to lower your goals. Learn to take it easy. Is anyone really comfortable in a model home? Magazines stacked perfectly just shows they aren't read!

Until the day comes that you put the oleo in the clothes hamper and the pajamas in the refrigerator (which one woman actually did), quit worrying. She laughed about it and so did I. She just had too much on her mind and too much to do.

The trick to making your house a home is to make fun out of housekeeping. Learn the short cuts and the easy way.

I would like to scream to the high heavens "Get rid of the clutter—if you don't use it, give it away, sell it, trade it or burn it." It's that simple.

If you haven't used something in a year, you probably never will. So why keep it? It just makes housekeeping more difficult. This is what we are trying to solve.

So think every time you do something and say to yourself, "Is there an easier way?" Nothing is so perfect that it can't be improved upon . . . .

And *don't* forget that I firmly believe in not working yourself to death. Many women have done just that and they are now six feet under.

Nobody sets your standards but *you! Not* your neighbor *or* your husband, your in-laws *or* your family. And if you are really smart, *don't* set theirs too high either! Each has his own troubles.

The friends who have written to tell me about their short cuts and hints were smart. They found an easier way. So as you read them—enjoy them and utilize them.

The backbone of any home is the wife. I hope every man understands that.

Always remember that your family comes *first!* Use your *best* silver and linens. There is no one who will ever be in your home who is *more* important.

And don't drink that second cup of coffee out of your everyday cup at the kitchen table after the family has left each morning.

Treat yourself to your *best* china cup and the living room chair for a few minutes . . . alone. Knowing housewives and mothers . . . this is probably the only time of the day you can be spoiled! And no one is going to spoil you but you yourself. So *let's do it.*

A great big God bless each of you. YOU are the very backbone of life itself.

Heloise

Thrifty Ways Are Best

BARGAIN DIVIDENDS

We all have our penny-pinching days. (This means that though we find something that's worth $25.00, we will not spend $2.00 for it.)

We also have our splurging days. (This means that no matter what it costs, we're going to buy it anyway!)

Once, when I happened to be on one of those tightfisted penny-pinching days, I saw a dress rack with a sign on it that said "Sale! Bargain! $1.99." I just had to stop and look. There were dresses worth up to $20.00 reduced to $1.99! Most of them were cotton, and they were large sizes!

So I said to myself, "I wear a size 12 and most of these

are 16's, 18's, 20's and 38's! Now if I took one of these dresses home, I would have to cut it up and completely remake it." Then I noticed that some of them had pleated skirts! I picked up one dress and, lo and behold, it had four yards of gorgeous material in it. Know what I did?

I bought that dress!

I came home, took my scissors and ripped it apart. First I salvaged the long zipper (which would have cost me at least 60 cents if I had bought it), the tape on the hem, and all the buttons and trimming!

I ripped off the voluminous skirt and made a housedress in my favorite pattern. Next, I cut the facings and plackets from the blouse of the dress. I took off the trim and put it on the pockets of my housedress. (After all, what's a housedress without pockets?)

The zipper I did not need, but some day I'll save 60 cents by using that zipper on another dress.

Ladies, always read the ads in your newspaper and look for the real bargains when you go to town.

DRESSES (ESPECIALLY COTTON) CAN BE REMADE into children's clothes, shorts, blouses and even men's sport shirts! Some prints make darling little girls' clothes. There is usually enough material if you find a dress that has lots of pleats.

I could not possibly have bought the material in the skirt of that dress for less than $8.00. Now I have a beautiful housedress for practically nothing.

So don't hesitate to look over that bargain counter when you see a sale. It will pay in the long run.

TOP VALUE FOR FOOD DOLLARS

To help stretch that FOOD BUDGET as far as possible,

learn to test different products yourself. Don't keep on buying the same brand just because you have been doing so for years.

Let's take canned tomatoes, for instance: They come in various sizes, grades and prices.

Your choice depends on what you are going to use them for. If it's for a spaghetti sauce, a cheaper grade does nicely. If the tomatoes have a hard core, just squeeze them and pick out the cores.

Stewing may require a better grade of tomatoes, or you may use the cheaper ones and remove the hard cores.

Don't be fooled by pretty labels on cans of food. Just because one brand of peas looks so nice and green on the label, doesn't mean they are like that inside the can. One brand I tested had an awful-looking label, but the peas were a lush green when opened.

Buy several different brands at a time in SMALL cans—then try them out. Compare quality, amount in the can, and price before you buy your next supply of peas. By opening two small cans, instead of one large one, it may cost a few cents more today. But you might also change brands next time. This also works with tuna fish, etc.

If you will test the above method, you might learn how you can get more for your money while meeting your family's needs.

If you do your marketing once a week, as I do, watch for bargains. (Read the ads in your paper and compare prices.)

Let's say there's a clearance of BAKED GOODS.

Figure it this way: If you buy boxes of doughnuts, sweet rolls, etc., you're not going to eat them all in one day, are you? So, what to do?

Buy several packages. As soon as you return home, open the packages, remove the contents, and mix them up. For instance, put a few sweet rolls, chocolate covered doughnuts, powdered doughnuts, etc., together in one package, and put it in your deepfreezer.

This way you will have a variety of mixed fresh buns, doughnuts, and sweet rolls when you need them, instead of having to eat doughnuts three days in succession. I have been told by bread-manufacturing companies that when you take most baked goods direct from the packages, rewrap them and place in your freezer, they do not age!

I have used this idea for our family for years—it's wonderful!

BUDGET DELECTABLES

From Tennessee: "Those who are on budgets and use lots of COFFEE will find that drip-grind goes lots further and makes stronger coffee. You can use the drip-grind in all kinds of pots, not just dripolators."

From Pennsylvania: "My five grandchildren enjoy POPCORN at the drive-in movie, so my daughter makes it at home, puts it in individual one-pound coffee cans, writes their names on the plastic lids, and away they go."

Sure saves on the budget; each child has his own container, and if he eats only half a can, the lid can be popped back on, thus saving spills in the car!

MATERIAL SAVINGS

From Montana: "I bought a round dinette set and found myself with many tablecloths of the wrong size and shape for it.

7

"On shopping around, I found the only round cloths of the size I needed were too expensive, so I decided to use a flowered bed sheet, size 81" x 108".

"I cut off one end (the one with the wide hem), and by cutting this strip in half and sewing just two seams in each, had a lovely pair of pillow slips.

"Then, with a pencil on a string, I traced and cut a circle fifteen inches larger than my table. I hemmed the circle and sewed ball fringe around it.

"I still had enough from the edges of the sheet for four small napkins which I fringed out on the edges.

"Result: One large round TABLECLOTH, one pair of pretty PILLOW SLIPS, and four luncheon-size NAPKINS for less than five dollars."

From Florida: "I made BABY BIBS out of cotton flannel-backed oilcloth. The bibs are washable, can be thrown in the dryer, and are absolutely safe for baby. No worry about any plastic adhering to his face. Best of all, the bib can be washed off after each use, as one would any plastic bib.

"A yard of oilcloth (cotton flannel-backed) can be purchased for about a dollar, and will make at least six bibs.

"They make lovely gifts, too."

MAKE THINGS LAST

Mothers, try this: When buying new PAJAMAS FOR CHILDREN, get a size larger than required. Then thread elastic through the hems at wrists and ankles. Later, when the children need the larger size, just remove the elastic!

From New York: "The soles on my TERRY CLOTH SLIPPERS used to wear out long before the slippers.

"Now I buy iron-on patches, cut them to the right size, and iron them to the soles of my house shoes. The slippers last twice as long."

From Texas: "After wearing out one CANVAS GLOVE each time I bought a pair (the right hand always seems to wear out first), I wash them and turn the complete pair inside out.

"This puts the less-worn left glove on the other hand, thus making a pair of gloves last much longer."

Whenever you buy a BLANKET, stitch a line, as close to the edge as possible, across the satin binding. No more split edges and the binding will look nice for years.

A golf pro in Virginia uses this method to prolong the life of GOLF SHOES: "Take paste-type floor wax and apply it to the bottoms and around the edges of the soles of your golf shoes. This prevents dampness from penetrating into the soles of the shoes and rusting the cleats.

"Keep the wax rag in your golf bag and use it on the soles and cleats after the game. Golf shoes will last at least twice as long!

"This method can also be used on the bottoms of golf bags and it also works beautifully on golf carts."

To make a BROOM last much longer, take an old nylon stocking, cut off the foot, double the leg section and pull it over the broom straws, leaving just a few inches of the broom for sweeping.

This not only keeps the straws from falling out, but keeps the broom in perfect shape!

FAR FROM FINISHED

From Texas: "The custom-made TABLE PADS for our large dining room table were white originally, but as time went on they became discolored and a little worn.

"I covered them with adhesive-backed paper in a walnut pattern that matched our furniture.

"It was easy to do, and it has made the pads very attractive again.

"I like to use them under lace tablecloths, as the wood pattern gives the impression that there are no pads."

From Illinois: "I found that placing a strip of adhesive-backed paper across the bottom of a worn WINDOW SHADE made the shade look better than before.

"Just cut the strip the width of the shade, and stick it on. This strip can be wiped off easily when it becomes soiled."

From Virginia: "If you have a RUBBER STAMP that doesn't print clearly, turn on your hot-water faucet and let the hot water run over it a few minutes. Then scrub it with an old toothbrush, and rinse well. Soap or a detergent sometimes helps, but we didn't find it really necessary. The stamp will print like new again.

"Another idea: Your sponge-rubber stamp pad MIGHT be dirty. Did you know you can hold it under hot water, too, then put new ink on it?"

From New Jersey: "Have an old WHISKBROOM that has seen its last days? Cut the worn bristles off at a forty-five-degree angle, and lo and behold, if you don't have the greatest gadget imaginable!

"That little point sweeps out all sorts of places the vacuum can't."

OPERATION RESTORATION

Here is a hint for concealing HOLES IN BEDSPREADS: Since you cannot make a patch completely invisible, make it so conspicuous that no one will suspect that it is a patch! Just appliqué butterflies or flowers over the holes!

If too many of them are concentrated in one section of the spread, scatter a few extra appliqués in the blank areas to even up the distribution.

This is also a suggestion for patching blouses and dresses.

Don't spend your hard-earned money having a new strap (or handle) made for your purse until you read further . . . I am overjoyed to pass on this secret. I inherited a beautiful alligator purse, but the HANDLE OF THE PURSE WAS WORN. My husband called all over town trying to have another strap made. And were they expensive! Besides, the color didn't match.

He thought I should buy a new purse until he saw the prices. He also saw that most of them had metal chain handles.

I went to the dime store and spotted a beautiful assortment of chain-type necklaces for less than a dollar. One of these was the answer.

When you remove the strap on last year's purse, you will find that it has a "claw" that you can slip this chain into. Just insert a link and squeeze it back together with your pliers.

It's a knockout! Looks like this year's purse.

Also, the handles of white summer purses often become stained with lipstick or makeup, so why not give that purse a fresh look, too, with this inexpensive handle?

So, before you throw away your old purse, or try to rejuvenate it by replacing the handle, *DO* go look at the junk-jewelry counter next time you go through a store.

You just might be surprised at what you will find.

LESS COSTLY CLEAN-UP

From Illinois: "I do not throw away old SILVERWARE CLEANING RAGS. I put them in a capped fruit jar and keep it in my towel drawer next to the sink.

"When the silver starts to tarnish, especially the forks, I take the dry rag and rub the wet silverware and it cleans

beautifully. I can use these old rags for sever
and I find they will do a good job. It sure saves
ware polish."

From Texas: "For years I have been irked by ⌐ rust
that forms in SCOURING PADS, sometimes after using them
only once.

"Finally, I discovered that instead of dipping my scouring pad in water, I could dip the article to be cleaned in
the water, and then use the dry pad to clean it.

"By using this method I have been able to use the pads
until all the soap is gone, and they never become rusty."

"As a rarely-in-the-kitchen bachelor, I have a suggestion:

"Don't throw away used ALUMINUM FOIL. When wadded
or crushed together, it makes a very effective scouring pad
for pans and casseroles.

"I discovered this after burning a pot of beans and not
having any steel wool on hand.

"With a little soap, the wad of aluminum foil works
quite well."

From Massachusetts: "I have found an easy way to
make a container to prolong the life of SOAP PADS.

"I use a large plastic dishwashing detergent bottle. Be
sure it's the round type.

"I cut off the top part (about one and one-half inches),
and the bottom part (about three inches), and fitted the
top over the bottom.

"The cap makes a handle for the top. It works beautifully and looks attractive on the drainboard."

PRESTO CHANGO!

From California: "My worn-out CHENILLE BEDSPREAD lay on a shelf for months before I finally thought of a way to use the good parts of it. I made the cutest beach coat from that tired old spread! It is so soft and snug and dries much faster than my heavy terry cloth coat."

From Michigan: "I took a BATH TOWEL that had shrunk in the band near each end from being in a too-hot dryer and cut it in two. Because of the shrinkage, the band formed a perfect waistline, with the terry cloth gathered neatly below.

"I trimmed off the toweling above the band (saved these pieces for polishing shoes), and hemmed the bottom (where the towel was cut in half), sewed a ribbon on the ends of the 'waistband,' and presto—two aprons and two shoe-polishing cloths from an otherwise ruined towel."

From New Hampshire: "Tell those housewives not to throw away their OLD DRAPERIES without first taking into consideration that some of the material might still be good.

"Usually, the only place where nice drapes rot is the portion where the sun shines in through the window. The tops and bottoms are still lovely.

"I made the nicest housecoat I've ever had from the good portions of some old drapes.

"After cutting away the faded parts, I washed and ironed my imitation brocade remnants and just cut away.

"A lovely housecoat at no cost."

Cut the cuffs of worn-out RUBBER GLOVES into narrow strips. This will give you rubber bands that will last for quite some time.

14

Use the mate of a lost kid glove for MAKING LEATHER BUTTONS, so popular for sports clothes.

Cut leather circles and gather around old plastic buttons, or use metal button frames. You can cut strips of leather to trim pockets, too.

From Connecticut: "My teen-age daughter always had a batch of BOBBY SOCKS that had lost the elasticity in the tops.

"I cut off the tops where the wide ridges end and discard the foot part. This leaves me with a ribbed tube.

"I take a pair of scissors and slit the tube between two ribs, and this leaves me with a square of ribbed cloth.

"I crochet around the edge of this ribbed cloth with leftover crochet cotton, finishing it with a loop on one corner, thereby making a lovely dishcloth! The colored edge gives an added zip."

I am not one who crochets so I took my scissors and just whacked the ribbed parts! (One could use pinking shears) . . . And, my, does it scrub!

Another thing I learned was to save the foot part (they are usually discolored) for applying wax to floors, polishing the car, etc.

From Pennsylvania: "My husband carries his lunch to work and had broken so many vacuum bottles that I just had to do something about it.

"I finally solved this problem by cutting the foot off an old bobby sock and slipping the knitted top over the bottle before putting it in the lunch bucket.

"The sock top is easily washed, and we haven't had a BROKEN VACUUM BOTTLE since I started using this method."

THERE'S A NEW USE FOR EVERYTHING

From Oklahoma: "How is this for an idea?

"After discarding several old, battered TV snack tables (the inexpensive type with the removable tray), I found that the folding-leg bases were still as good as new.

"So when I needed a laundry cart, I made a bag of lightweight canvas and sewed it to the two top rims of the TV tables. Presto—a laundry cart!

"The stands with wheels are especially handy, but the others are good, too.

"Another thing I found out is that since these stands are lightweight you can use two or three at one time and thus divide your laundry as you work with it."

From New York: "I never throw away those dabs of cotton which come in the tops of medicine, pill and aspirin bottles. I save and use them for removing nail polish, as swabs, etc.

"These are kept with my first-aid kit in the kitchen—where most home accidents occur."

From Kentucky: "Handles off cups? Get hubby to sand them down, after knocking off the remainder of handle. You then have darling rice bowls or containers for leftovers. We've been doing this for years and even like to break cup handles now to get the tiny bowls!"

Don't throw away those envelopes from greeting cards that haven't been sealed.

I cut off the FLAPS FROM THE ENVELOPES and stow them in a small box.

When I have to leave a note, and don't want the piece

16

of paper to get pushed aside or lost, I just wet the glue
and stick the note up in plain sight.

These flaps are also good for labeling jams and jellies.

Did you realize that a roll of inexpensive wallpaper
makes WONDERFUL WRAPPING for games and other large
birthday presents?

SAVE THOSE PLASTIC BAGS

From Rhode Island: "I have found so many uses for
those WONDERFUL PLASTIC BAGS from the dry cleaner's.

"I cut them into small strips and use the strips to tie
plants to the stakes in our garden. The plastic will give a
little, not cut the stem of the plant, and is practically invisible.

"I use the bags to wrap items to be put in storage, such
as books, picture albums, lampshades, etc. The bags protect them from dust and moisture.

"I use them as drop cloths before painting, as the paint
will not seep through the plastic as it sometimes does when
using newspapers.

"I slip our folding lawn chairs into them for storing
in the fall, and put them up on the rafters (out of the reach
of children) in the garage. Keeps dust out of the canvas
and plastic seats."

This Rhode Islander has listed some wonderful uses for
the dry-cleaning bags, but I want to CAUTION you again:
Keep the bags out of the reach of children, and when you
are ready to discard them, knot them up TIGHTLY so that a
child cannot untie them.

From Arizona: "We have instant this and instant that—
so try these INSTANT CUSHIONS.

"Save (*in a safe place*) those soft PLASTIC DRY-CLEAN-ING COVERS. Use them to stuff some extra throw cushions.

"Most every housewife who sews has scraps of nice materials, large enough to stitch up cushion covers.

"These plastic bags make the nicest, lightest, softest stuffing, and the cushions fluff up instantly with a slight shake."

MORE TRICKS WITH PLASTICS

From South Carolina: "My son has found another use for empty plastic BLEACH CONTAINERS.

"He filled a half-gallon plastic jug with mortar, and when it hardened, he had a perfect boat anchor for his runabout. The handle on the jug is used to tie the anchor rope."

From Oregon: "Here's the perfect substitute for those worn-out glider tips on your dinette chairs:

"Save the correct size plastic SNAP-TYPE LIDS from your empty medicine bottles and just snap right over the bottom tips of corresponding-size chair legs.

"They fit perfectly, and the chairs will slide beautifully without scratching and making marks on your floor."

From Ohio: "PLASTIC COVERS from coffee cans are wonderful to use under small flowerpots. They can be dressed up by placing colored paper or foil between two covers. This also helps keep them from sweating.

"Best of all, these plastic covers won't scratch surfaces."

From Michigan: "I made an INSULATED BLANKET by sewing a piece of thin plastic between two sheet blankets.

I sewed around the edges and across several times to hold all three together firmly.

"It works as well as the most expensive insulated blanket."

From Indiana: "I find that small plastic bottles make fine FISHING FLOATS.

"All you do is screw the cap on over the fishing line."

From New Mexico: "For home movie fans: Don't discard the twenty-five-foot PLASTIC REELS that are left after you splice your films onto a larger reel.

"They are wonderful for winding on leftover bias tape, ribbon, crochet cotton, embroidery thread, and the like.

"The end of the tape can be pulled through a notch on the reel after winding, and it will not come undone.

"This makes for a neater sewing basket, and no more time is wasted fishing for the right thread, etc."

From Pennsylvania: "I discovered a fine use for the PLASTIC CONTAINERS in which tomatoes are packaged.

"Since most wall medicine cabinets have narrow shelves, bottles are easily upset when reaching for a certain article. I place these empty tomato cartons on the cabinet shelves and put medicine bottles inside them. No more tipping over!

"I also find that nothing sticks to the shelves now that I'm using these plastic containers. It's much easier to keep the cabinet clean."

From Vermont: "When my husband wanted to scrape the frost off the car windshield and couldn't find the

19

scraper, he used a PLASTIC COFFEE-CAN COVER. Believe it
or not, he found that it worked better than the regular
scraper. The cover bends in one's hand to fit the curve of
the windshield and peels off a good wide swath of frost at
each swipe."

THOSE WONDERFUL NYLONS

Here's one for the books:

If you will take four or five OLD NYLON STOCKINGS,
hold them up by the toes so they will all be the same
length, and tie them in a knot in the middle of the whole
kit and caboodle; then take your scissors and cut the feet
and tops off all the same length (as long as you want 'em),
you'll have the niftiest scouring rag you ever saw!

These free mops are just wonderful for washing the tub,
scouring all the fixtures, and, best of all, for washing
dishes!

They don't sour or smell, and they make a wonderful
cleaning rag when scouring the sink with cleansing powders, etc.

You can make these helpy-selfy gadgets with as many,
or as few, old nylons as you wish. You can cut the ends as
long or as short as your little heart desires, too.

Another thing I discovered is that you can take an old
nylon, tie a knot above the ankle, fill it full of shredded
nylons (cut some up in strips with your scissors), tie another knot, cut the end off, and have the greatest little
padded thingumajig you ever saw!

This can be used for so many things. It's a dilly for
washing the car! Doesn't scratch at all, can be rinsed like
lightning, and is so lightweight that it handles like a bubble.

This little dream is wonderful for taking a bath! Real
invigorating!

But the best part of it all is that it's absolutely free. So why not at least try it?

From Indiana: "Don't throw away a HOT-WATER BOTTLE that has sprung a leak.

"Just stuff it with old nylon stockings, press the air out and screw in the stopper.

"Then see what a fine kneeling pad you have for gardening! Can be washed in a jiff, too."

From Ohio: "I wear STOCKINGS all the time, so I buy them by the dozen for everyday wear . . . all alike, same size and shade.

"On washday, I have six or eight pairs to wash. After drying, I just fold any two together, and they match.

"When I discover a runner in one when wearing them, I pull that stocking off *wrong side out*.

"In folding up the pairs, if one is wrong side out, I know it has a run, so I put it in a bag.

"When I have several, I make a mop by tying them together and fastening to a handle. Works just fine."

WASTE NOT

From a man in Illinois: "TO CONSERVE WATER, whether in a water-shortage area, or just in the average home, may I tell you how we in the Navy were taught to shower, using the least amount of water?

"Turn on the water, and after wetting down, turn the water off. Then put some soap on a wet wash cloth, and bathe away.

"Then turn on the shower to rinse yourself off.

"This method takes only about two gallons of water, whereas an ordinary shower uses seven or more gallons because the average person turns the shower on full blast.

"A tub bath uses about ten gallons of H_2O.

"Some saving!"

From Nevada: "With most HAIR SPRAYS, one must spray on more after combing the hair.

"Instead of building up spray on my hair in this way, I take a clean, pushbutton spray bottle (such as some window cleaners come in), and fill it with water.

"After spraying my hair with hair spray once, I can renew it several times just by dampening it with water from the spray bottle."

From Connecticut: "I was becoming unhappy about my FLASHLIGHT BATTERIES going dead when I did not use the flashlight, so I decided to do something about it.

"I inserted the last battery in reverse position. Then when I want to use the flashlight, all I have to do is to turn the battery to the right position.

"Now I always have a good light."

From Texas: "Here's something that might save some of our friends some money:

"If you have a tape recorder or transistor radio that works on BATTERIES (most contain four), and you think you need to replace all of the batteries, try this first.

"Remove only one battery at a time, and insert a new one. If this doesn't change the speed, sound, etc., most likely the one you removed is still good! Put it back, and continue from there. Most times, all you need is one new battery, not four!

"Also, often the end of a battery can be sanded with an emery board or a piece of sandpaper, thus bringing better contact through all batteries. This also works in multiple-battery flashlights."

This is to all of you who buy expensive MOISTURIZER LOTIONS IN SMALL-NECKED GLASS BOTTLES.

Once you think you have gotten all you can out of the bottle, recap and set it upside down under the hot-water faucet, letting the hot water run over it for a few minutes.

Remove the jar, leaving it capped, and let it stand upside down for a while. When you open it, there will be enough moisturizer in the cap to last you another several days, and the bottle will be clean as a whistle.

This also works on other products that come in plastic or glass jars.

Chef Savers

I think we gals spend more time in the kitchen than any other place in the house. Agreed? Well, we all spend more time than we need to, no matter how efficient we are. You'll spend less, I guarantee, if you put the time- and fuss-savers in the following pages into practice.

The other important aspect of kitcheneering is money. No one needs to tell you that the drain on the food-budget purse strings is harder than ever. Believe me, you can economize and still serve nutritious, exciting meals. Read on and see if I'm not right!

BE A CHEESE WIZARD

Some time ago, a woman told us the most wonderful hint: To grate cheese as soon as we bring it home from the store and put it in plastic bags in the freezer.

24

The grandest thing about this GRATED CHEESE is that you can always remove the exact amount you need. The cheese doesn't stick together when frozen and it thaws instantly. So why dirty your grater each time you need a bit of cheese when you can shred it all at once?

I think I have uses for this grated cheese that you will all love, especially when you are on a tight budget.

Try sprinkling some on a lettuce and tomato sandwich. All you do is spread some mustard or mayonnaise (and if you mix the two, it's even better) on some bread or toast. Add your sliced tomato and lettuce and some grated cheese. Then add anything else you want, such as pickles or a dash of celery salt.

Make it thick!

When you bite into the sandwich à la Heloise, it's so tender.

And know what else?

You can also spread the mustard mixture on a piece of bread, put sliced pickles on it, add a couple of slices of tomato and broil it for a few minutes. Pile some grated cheese on top of the broiled tomato.

At this time, lay a topper (that's another piece of bread) in the broiler so it will toast on one side, and as soon as the grated cheese melts, put the topper on . . . toasted side down. Easier to eat! It's marvelous.

Here are some variations you can use with cooked, leftover sausage, ham or breakfast bacon. If you have only one or two pieces of bacon, cut them up and sprinkle the pieces over the tomato. Just cook under broiler with everything except the cheese. Then toss the finely grated cheese on top!

Another thing I have found is that the grated cheese makes a wonderful cold lunch for those who carry lunches.

Here's how to do it: Put mustard, butter (I use oleo) or mayonnaise on your bread, add a piece of lettuce, then add that frozen grated cheese and pile it high! By the time noon comes, the cheese is thawed. Oh, it's so different. The sandwich will stand up twice as high. It's light, puffy and invigorating . . . nothing like a plain slice of cheese.

And grated cheese goes *much* further, no matter what brand you buy. Try it!

From Alaska: "When I want TO GRATE A SMALL AMOUNT OF CHEESE I use my vegetable peeler. It's much handier to reach for and easier to wash than a grater."

"For GRATED CHEESE without a sticky mess on the grater, put the piece of cheese in your freezer for thirty or forty minutes.

"It then grates firmly—no fuss, and much quicker."

THE BOILED EGG BIT

From New York: "When you have a large family, everyone wants his BOILED EGGS cooked a different length of time.

"I write the name of each member of the family on an egg, and how many minutes they like to have their egg cooked.

"Then I set my timer and just put the eggs into the water —eggs to be hard-boiled go in first, medium-boiled second, and soft-boiled last.

"It is easy to separate the eggs after cooking because the pencil marks do not disappear, and remember, there is only one pan to wash!

"Everybody is pleased, and the younger members of the family are quite thrilled with their personalized eggs."

From Arizona: "I have an easy way TO PEEL HARD-BOILED EGGS. Here's how: Just pour the hot water off, and immediately shake the pan vigorously (with the eggs still in it) until they're all well cracked. Then pour cold water on them.

"Now, watch them practically slide right out of their shells.

"This sure eliminates work, and saves time."

From Ohio: "To PREVENT HARD-BOILED EGGS FROM CRACKING, pierce a tiny hole in the large end of the egg before putting it in the water. (It is the air inside that causes the egg to crack.)

"Make yourself a needle gadget: Take a long needle, hold it in the center with a pair of pliers and push the eye end into a large cork.

"This is also excellent for testing vegetables for 'doneness' because it won't split the vegetable the way a fork tine sometimes does.

"I stick the point of the needle into a smaller cork to keep from pricking my finger when it is in the drawer."

POACHED EGGS PRONTO

From Illinois: "If you are fixing POACHED EGGS FOR A LARGE FAMILY, try using your cupcake-baking tin.

"Put the tin in a flat baking pan which has been half-filled with cold water, put a dab of butter into each tin to be used, cook on a slow burner on your stove, and the eggs will come out evenly cooked . . . all at one time! You may want to cover the cupcake pan with foil; however, I don't bother.

"You may have to use two burners at once, depending on the size pan you are using."

GARLIC AS YOU LIKE IT

For perfect GARLIC OIL, folks, buy some dried garlic. Break all the buds apart.

Cut off the end and top of each bud. Then peel with your paring knife. (It will peel just like an onion.) Cut each little bud in half, drop them all in a bottle, and cover them with oil!

Within one day the oil is so terrifically "garlicked" that you will need only a few drops for your recipe. Can be used in spaghetti, chicken, salads, etc.

When making vinegar and oil dressing for salads, add a few (and you better believe it—I MEAN a few) drops of the oil.

If more oil is added to the garlic buds from time to time, they will last for ages. I keep them in a tightly-capped bottle in the refrigerator.

And did you all know you can always have FRESH GARLIC with a minimum of effort?

Just put an unpeeled bud of garlic, root end down, in a glass with a bit of water, leave it for about three days until roots appear; then plant it in a small pot of soil. Empty condiment shakers are good for this.

The garlic will grow about a foot high, and, as you need it, you can just break off a piece (looks like chives!) and chop it to use in soups, spaghetti sauces, salads, etc. Dee-lishus!

And, simple!

HAMBURGER MEAT (Ground Beef)

As far as I am concerned, ground beef (hamburger) is the most popular meat in the entire universe because it has so many uses.

For the family who is cost conscious, I suggest that you buy the ADVERTISED ground beef at the lowest possible price from legitimate meat or supermarkets. Then learn some fantastic ways to make it different. Many unique ways you can make up yourself.

Here are some that I have tried over the last six months, and have found perfect:

No matter what you pay for that pound of ground beef, and PROVIDED that it DOES NOT CONTAIN FILLER (you will know if it has filler because it feels different when you try to make a patty for a hamburger or sometimes it's discolored before cooking), here is the way to make it taste better:

Take one beef bouillon cube (The bouillon cube has all the necessary flavoring plus the seasoning!) and put it in a cup, pour a teaspoonful of boiling water over the cube and let set a minute or so. Then take a spoon and mash it HARD and you will be left with about a tablespoonful of liquid beef bouillon.

Pour this into one pound of ground beef. Mix it well so it will distribute evenly. And see and taste for your little ol' self how different the flavor is. It will have a heavy beef flavor.

This may be used in meat patties, meatballs, for spaghetti sauce or that good old American standby—meatloaf.

No matter what you use it for—it's so much more flavorful.

And another little dilly I would like to pass along:

Try using chicken bouillon cubes in place of the beef cubes. I find them so different and good. Sure changes the taste.

I have also mixed one beef cube and one chicken cube and it's even better.

Another thing I would like to tell all of you who use ground meat (again, with no extenders):

Grate a BIG onion in a mixing bowl. This will have liquid . . . after all, water is a large percent of onion. Put liquid and all in your pound of ground meat and squeeze and mix it with your hand. My, does this change its taste. (Sometimes I add Worcestershire or some other sauce just to vary the taste.)

Do NOT use this the same day. Wrap it in plastic wrap and let it set at least 24 hours in your refrigerator.

Then make your very own recipe from there. It's absolutely out of this world for Salisbury steak, hamburgers, meatballs or spaghetti sauce. The raw grated onion absorbs into the meat itself, and you would never know it was just plain old hamburger at all.

MORE GOODIES IN GROUND MEAT

From New York: "Would you like a spatter-proof method of FRYING HAMBURGERS?

"Form the patties in any way, shape or form you like, then flour them on both sides before frying them.

"Not only will this prevent spattering, but the flour seals in the meat juices, gives the patties a thin, crispy crust and helps them retain their shape.

"We often buy hamburger on sale, make the patties and

flour them. Then we wrap them individually in waxed paper and stack them in the freezer for future use."

"If you have to make that pound of hamburger stretch when making your MEAT LOAF, try adding some precooked rice!

"This is especially good when it's a bit soppy or soft to mold. Gives it lots of body!"

From Pennsylvania: "When we make 'BURGER-DOGS' (hamburgers in the shape of hot dogs and served on hot dog buns), I add a strip of bacon, coiled around the hamburger-dog, and broil it.

"The bacon adds flavor, and makes the burger-dog better than either hamburgers or hot dogs!"

"When GRINDING LEFTOVER ROAST and the recipe calls for chopped onions, I grind the onion along with the meat. This way the onion is evenly mixed throughout the meat, and the juice adds flavor. Also saves time."

I wonder if you have ever tried putting DRIED ONION SOUP MIX into plain ol' hamburger meat and mixing it well before making those hamburgers, Salisbury steaks, or meat loaves?

One doesn't have to use a whole package either. First time, try about a quarter of a package of mix to each pound of hamburger. It surely gives hamburger meat a new lift and taste.

HOW TO STRETCH HAMBURGER

Also I want to talk to you about ground meat (hamburger) and its s-t-r-e-t-c-h-e-r-s. . . .

And my, can you stretch a pound IF it hasn't already got filling or stretcher in it.

Ask your meat market man BEFORE you buy it. If he turns red (the color of the hamburger!) or blushes, you know it has.

Now, remember that we told you to put a spoonful of water over a bouillon cube, and when it dissolves, mix it well into your pound of meat.

And those of you who are on a strict budget can always add what the meat industry calls "Extenders." These extenders make a pound of hamburger weigh more and it goes further. That's why I call 'em s-t-r-e-t-c-h-e-r-s.

After talking with a reputable meat packer, I learned just what extenders are, what CAN and should be used, and the things that CANNOT be added to hamburger because they show or just won't mix.

An extender is something we add to ground meat that blends into the meat, and when it's cooked it seems to have disappeared, and the meat looks like ALL meat. In other words, it doesn't show anything has been added. Some things that you add to ground meat will NOT disappear when cooked. This shows that extenders have been added.

So, you can see there is really a big difference.

Naturally, some things we do not want to disappear— such as grated carrots—because they add color, etc.

Ground or finely crushed corn flakes, or any other cereal that suits your taste, such as oatmeal (precooked or raw), bread crumbs, cracker crumbs, packaged turkey stuffing which contains sage (and that is wonderful . . . wow!) can be blended into the hamburger and will disappear when it's cooked.

Now, here are some hints on what NOT to use because

they won't blend with the meat without showing when it's cooked—if that's what you want:

Regular farina . . . just plain won't blend.

Rice will show up in the cooking as a separate ingredient.

So, don't forget, gals, try those wonderful stretchers and extenders. They're quite worthy in my book.

Use them along with the bouillon cubes. (And I often wonder why somebody doesn't make HAM bouillon cubes.)

And don't forget to try that packaged turkey stuffing. If you can't afford it, save your bread and use that for stretching, and when you add your liquid to your meat loaf, just put a dab or so of sage into the liquid, then squeeze and mix away. And don't ask me how much a "dab" is! Just use it according to your own taste.

You can also use poultry seasoning instead of sage. I sometimes mix both together.

Anyway, here's to it. I do suggest that you try these meat extenders.

Last night, I put chili powder (one teaspoonful) with some grated onions in my pound of hamburger meat, and it was a knockout!

Sort of gave it the flavor of barbecue. Imagine!

TENDERIZE MEAT

There are so many different ways to buy meat that I couldn't begin to shake a stick at one-tenth of them!

But let me tell you something I have learned about round and cube steak, especially when you see a sale and want to stock up your freezer.

Did you know that you could pick out a round steak from the counter (ring that little bell in some stores), and have the butcher tenderize it for you free? He will!

This means that he will run it through a gadget with tiny claws, such as our meat pounders. I always have mine run through twice as this makes it twice as tender, and far more edible.

When you get home, cut that big steak into serving portions, then put each portion in one of those new plastic sandwich bags. They don't cost very much; but if you feel you can't afford them, use ordinary plastic. I *always* put tenderizer on the top of the meat, then wrap and freeze it.

Let me tell you why:

I feel that since your meat is not frozen, the tenderizer works while it is freezing, and when you remove it from the freezer, it works *again* while it thaws!

I am positive of this, as I have tested it for over a year.

Another thing, did you know that you could use tenderizer not only on steaks, but also on chicken, lamb and liver? Yes, you can. So long may tenderizer wave!

After you put your meats into these little plastic bags, you can take your fist and hit the wrapped piece of meat, and it will shape to the plastic package beautifully.

By placing these individual portions in separate wrapping, they are easily separated and thaw quickly. (Ever need something to prepare in a hurry? Especially when that extra guest arrives?) These store beautifully in an ice tray if you don't have a freezer.

Just watch your ads in the paper, and buy hunks of good meat when it's on sale.

FROZEN FISH STICKS

Ladies, you know those frozen fish sticks we buy once in a while?

Don't put them in a pan and cook them.

Save a piece of foil you have used for something else, and washed and set aside. I always put these extra pieces of foil back in my oven (I have the gas-type with a pilot light) so that it will dry them.

Another thing about keeping these extra pieces of foil in your oven is that you remember to use them.

Now, back to the fish sticks . . . put your fish sticks on this piece of crumpled foil (that means it's wadded, crooked, all squashed up and then slightly smoothed out).

Your fish sticks will get brown on the bottom the same time they do on the top! They can be turned over with the flip of a fork, never stick, never are gooey on one side and brown on the other, and it's absolutely fantabulous.

Try it.

ONIONS

A home economist wrote that if you would turn on the back burner of your gas stove when cutting onions you would not cry. It works, too!

If you breathe through your mouth instead of your nose when chopping onions you won't cry either. Some people put a toothpick or piece of bread in their mouth so they will remember to keep it open (our husbands will love that!). The reason for this is:

Since you are not breathing through your nose the onion odor does not reach the tear-producing glands.

Too, rubber gloves can always be worn to keep the odor off your hands or if the onion is chilled in the refrigerator a few days or so . . . it cannot possibly smell at all. Unbelievable? Try it.

35

SOAKING BEANS

"If I forget to soak beans overnight, is there any way to soften them to shorten the cooking time and save on utilities?

"I am on such a tight budget. Please help me."

M-m-m . . . I love beans!

When I forget to put them in to soak the night before, I just sort them, put them in my colander and wash them under the hot water faucet. You'll find half of these "rocks" weren't rocks at all but hard bits of dirt.

After they are washed, put them in a pot and cover with enough water to come about three inches above the beans. Put the cover on and bring to a boil for five minutes.

Now turn out your fire. This is where you will save on the utility bill.

DON'T remove the cover. Let the beans set an hour or two.

Then I usually pour off this water and replace it with fresh water, add my seasonings and cook 'em from there.

Beans (any kind) are delicious when sliced onions or canned tomatoes are added.

Never, NEVER add salt until a few minutes before you are ready to serve them. This is what causes them to be hard as rocks.

SNAPPED GREEN BEANS

I have snapped green beans for 25 years. . . .

Recently, for the first time, I learned a quicker, more sanitary way. (I was in such a hurry that I had to figure out something!)

I filled my sink with cold water, dunked the whole two

pounds of string beans in the water, and sloshed them around with my hands. You should have seen the soil that was in that whole sinkful of water. I never knew beans had so much soil before.

Very carefully, I tilted the stopper in the sink, and let this water drain out. Then I replaced the stopper, turned on the cold water faucet full force, and let the sink fill half full again. When I looked at that water! We don't always know how much dust the beans have on 'em until we use this method.

Now, here is what is going to surprise you. Your beans will literally float on top of the water! Land o'Goshen, within one-third of the time it usually takes you to snap those beans, you can get it done this way:

Gently turn on the cold water faucet, pick up a string bean with the left hand, hold it under the faucet, and snap both ends off.

Drop each broken end back into the sink.

Put the snapped string beans in the water in your cooking vessel. There is absolutely no need to break string beans into small pieces. Are you aware that canned whole string beans cost more?

After all the beans are snapped, gather up the ends and culls and discard them. If you have a disposal, you are lucky. Turn it on!

Drain the beans and fill the cooking vessel once more with water, pour this off for a last thorough rinsing, then add the necessary amount of water and seasoning to cook the beans.

You have saved one-third the time by using this new method of snapping beans, because the cold water makes them so crisp they snap much faster.

TURKEY DRESSING

We all love our good ol' turkey dressing along with all the trimmings . . . and one reason most of us fail to make the good old-fashioned kind is that it takes so long and it is always eaten in one or two days.

So we think, "Why should I work so hard for a meal or two?"

Well, let me tell you how to capitalize on this sort of cooking, which takes so much time.

Make lots of dressing! Double your recipe (I triple mine) and make it good while you are at it.

Not only will it taste better, but eeks! . . . think of the energy you will save next time you wish you had some dressing and don't have the time or inclination, or all the ingredients in the house to make it.

I use the old-fashioned recipe of homemade cornbread, homemade biscuits, etc., so I know what you go through but I sure don't waste any energy because, after making up a whole batch, I use it many ways.

I set aside as much as I think I will need for the immediate meal and cook this when I get ready to bake my turkey.

The portion that is left I use in two different ways after I cook it. If you make your dressing a day ahead of time, cook the remaining dressing then, because you will not have room in your oven the day you bake your turkey. Let this cool.

Figure out how much it takes for your family for one meal. Put this in a pie tin that has been lined with foil and press the dressing flat. When dressing is flat, it not only freezes faster but thaws more quickly!

I sometimes cover this with some gravy before freezing

it. Makes it moist and yummy. Cover with foil and freeze.

Next time you buy a small turkey or roasting hen, your dressing is ready! It is also lush when reheated and served with pork chops and gravy. Just thaw and reheat.

Now for the second way . . . and you are going to get the surprise of your life when you try this!

Moisten the remainder of the cooked dressing with a little water, leftover broth or cold gravy and mold it into little portions about the size and shape of medium-sized baking potatoes.

Then wrap these in pieces of foil (just as you would for baking potatoes) and put them in your freezer. These may be served with anything in place of a baked potato.

Now . . . the greatest thing about these little foil-covered dressing balls is that you can use as many or as few of them as you need when the occasion arises. And with no waste at all. Besides, they take up very little space in your freezer, because they can be tucked into all those little wasted spaces.

Without thawing, I rebake them in the oven (350°) for 40 minutes or so (according to the size), to heat them clear through. (Sometimes I thaw them before reheating; it's faster because they don't *have* to bake so long, but they are not as crisp on the outside.)

I cut a big "X" in these dressing balls, through foil and all, just as one does a baked potato, and top it with a pat of butter or some gravy. Yum, yum. The part next to the foil is real crispy, and the inside is nice and moist. Looks lovely on your dinner plate too.

So, don't hesitate to make lots of good dressing when you bake your turkey this year. It's surely nice to just open the freezer and pick up those packages of dressing balls a few weeks later.

39

And here's another little hint for warm leftover dressing from that dinner table:

While it's still warm . . . stuff it in a big jelly glass and mash it down hard. Put in refrigerator. In the next few days remove this with a knife. It will slide out beautifully.

Cut this in portions about an inch thick. These patties may either be laid on a piece of foil and rebaked, or dipped in flour and fried for breakfast! Fabulous.

MERINGUE

A nice old lady taught me this:

"To keep meringue from falling on pies, of course bake it slowly, but as soon as the pie is removed from the oven, dip a thin knife in hot water and cut through the meringue, NOT the whole pie, in serving pieces."

After trying this hint, I found I loved the idea of cutting through the meringue while the pie was still hot! Amazing when that knife was dipped in hot water how clean it cut through my warm meringue.

Now here are a few more hints that I have learned about meringue from famous bakers in three fabulous hotels:

Egg whites should always be room temperature before beating. And use a minimum of three eggs for each pie.

After they are beaten stiff but NOT dry, sprinkle one-fourth teaspoon cream of tartar and a dash of salt on top and beat slightly.

Now . . . add S L O W L Y three level tablespoonfuls of sugar for each egg white in your bowl, beating all the while. This sounds like a lot, I know, but you should see the difference in the height of your meringue and the way it stands up after the pie is done . . . wow!

Professional bakers have proven to me that the following must be observed before baking:

Always have your meringue touching the edges of the piecrust. This prevents shrinking, etc.

If the pie is put on the middle shelf (NOT the top) in your oven, it will brown evenly and the points or swirls on your meringue won't get burned.

When it is ALMOST as brown as you want it, if you turn off your oven and open the door SLIGHTLY, it will cool slowly; this prevents a meringue from cracking or splitting.

Don't ever set a pie where cold drafts can get to it while it's hot. It must be cooled slowly.

And most important of all (which I have saved till last, so that you will remember it):

NEVER put a meringue on a pie or use it anywhere else until you have tested it to see if the sugar is COMPLETELY DISSOLVED before cooking. The way to do this is to put some of it between two fingertips and rub them together.

Or (as I have just learned), it is even better to put a little of it on the tip of your tongue, rub it on the roof of your mouth and feel the undissolved sugar. "Chew" the meringue and you can even hear it grate between your teeth!

If you feel grains of sugar . . . believe it, you better keep beating some more. The grains should be COMPLETELY dissolved before cooking, as this is one of the causes of "tears" on a pie. Either your eggs weren't room temperature, or you haven't beaten 'em enough.

And that's all I've stolen from the good chefs and cooks about pie meringue!

Bless 'em all.

P. S. And when I asked each chef if his wife cooked pies and goodies, the answer was, "Heavens, NO! Why should she?"

SALMONETTES HELOISE

Here's something I discovered quite by accident while trying to salvage a can of salmon after testing another recipe. And believe me, you won't even know you are eating salmon!

Here's all it takes:

1. One 15-ounce can of pink salmon (lots cheaper than red)
2. One whole egg
3. One HEAPING teaspoon of baking powder
4. One-half cup of flour
5. *Only* about five minutes of *your time* from start to finish! (And what else can you cook that fast that's really good—and cheap, too?)

Now . . . here's how:

Open your can of salmon. Pour the juice into a measuring cup and *set aside*. Dump the drained salmon in a mixing bowl. Drop in one whole egg.

Use fork to break up salmon and mix the egg real good. When it's gummy, add a half cup of sifted flour. Stir in flour thoroughly with fork again. This mixture will be real thick. Don't worry . . . it's supposed to be that way!

DON'T add any salt. Pepper is OK.

Take one-fourth cup of the salmon juice (pour out any excess—brands of salmon differ in liquid content) and add one HEAPING teaspoon of baking powder to the juice and beat with a fork. It's going to foam. Good. Supposed to. Your measuring cup should be three-quarters full of foam! This is what makes the difference in your recipe! If it doesn't foam your baking powder may be old.

42

After the foaming process has worked, pour this into your salmon mixture. Mix again with that fork. It's going to be really thin this time. That's the secret to it all. . . .

Pick up two ice tea spoons (you have to use a small spoon) and dip a half spoonful of this luscious stuff and scoop it out with the other spoon into a deep fryer half-full of hot oil.

And gals, the scoops of batter don't have to be perfect. The "crookeder" they are the better.

These tidbits don't even have to be turned. They will float on top of the hot oil! They turn themselves as they cook and are completely done in just a few seconds.

Your luscious brown tidbits will look as if you have dipped them into a secret, time-consuming, lacy batter and the crust browns beautifully. Another funny thing about it is they aren't greasy.

All I can figure out is the effervescence (bubbles) which I got from the mixture of the salmon juice and the baking powder (why, we never figured out) seems to be what makes them light, lacy and crunchy . . .

When you look at your completed tidbit, you can actually see a lace design on the outside. This is the best part of it. Most amazing thing I ever saw!

This batter CANNOT be made ahead of time and saved. It must be cooked within 15 minutes after mixing in the foamy baking powder and juice.

So don't hesitate to splurge on a can of salmon. SALMON-ETTES HELOISE will absolutely melt in your mouth with a delicious crunch. The outside crust will be as lacy as fine old Alençon.

It's not only quick to make, but cooks in seconds and is quite inexpensive in the long run because it expands and expands and expands . . .

This recipe can be varied by adding grated onions, garlic salt, etc. Wonderful for parties when stuck with a toothpick and served with or without a dip. Or pile 'em up on a plate for supper and serve with a hot sauce over them.

And you know what else? They're even great cold the next day. And what housewife doesn't like a quickie good lunch most days?

BETTER PEANUT BUTTER

From Vermont: "Try mixing maple or waffle syrup in your PEANUT BUTTER.

"It will not tear the slices of bread when spread and is delicious."

From Kentucky: "I eat PEANUT BUTTER AND JELLY SANDWICHES for lunch, and my mother sometimes finds the peanut butter difficult to spread.

"So one day she put the peanut butter on when the bread was frozen. I tried it, too. It spread much better and didn't tear the bread apart."

POTATO SENSATIONS

Some time ago, a woman wrote and suggested that I cut a big BAKING POTATO in half, and insert a large, thick slice from a cooking onion between the halves before wrapping it in foil and baking it.

It's out on Cloud Nine again! (I wish we lived there, don't you?)

I cut my big slice of onion nearly a half-inch thick, but you can slice yours thinner if you like.

I also learned to salt and pepper both cut halves of the potato before baking it.

Garlic salt in place of the salt and pepper is a knockout, too, but be sure to serve this only on weekends, if you don't want your husband going to work with garlic breath next day!

When this onion-potato is served, cut a big X through the foil and skin, and either mash it a little bit or use a fork to break up the center, so your butter or sour cream will go down into the spud.

The aroma and taste are out of this world. Why not give this a whirl some day when you are in the potato-baking mood?

From Utah: "To hurry BAKED POTATOES, I place them on the rack in my oven and put an iron utensil over them. This cuts the baking time almost in half!"

From Ohio: "When my FRENCH FRIES are done, I put them into a large, clean, brown paper bag and shake them. As the potatoes come in contact with the sides of the bag, the paper absorbs most of the grease. Saves paper toweling and can be done in a jiffy.

"Also, when I have to fry more than one batch, the paper bag helps to keep the first batch warm."

When making POTATO SALAD, cut the raw potatoes into

bite-size pieces before cooking them. They are cooked in minutes and ready to use immediately.

After draining them, try pouring your favorite dressing mixture over the potatoes while they are still hot! Wow! The potatoes absorb the condiments beautifully. It's out of this world, too!

SOUR PICKLE SECRET

Question: Just how does one get REALLY SOUR, SOUR PICKLES today? Please answer as our whole family are sour bugs!

Answer: I have checked with a top pickle man in the business and he gave me his terrific special recipe that I will share with you. And, gals, these are really sour, so watch your step before you bite off too big a chunk!

Buy processed (read fine print on bottle) or genuine dill pickles and pour off the juice.

Slice the pickles any shape you wish—crosswise or lengthwise, in thin slices or stick-style.

Put pickles back in the jar and fill the jar with distilled WHITE vinegar. Be sure it's five percent acidity.

Put the top back on the bottle and let it set at room temperature for three days. After that the pickles MUST be kept under refrigeration.

Wow! Talk about a sour pickle . . . It's great!

PIZZA, PLEASE!

From New Jersey: "My family loves PIZZA. The boys, especially, like the individual ones.

"I had some cans of dinner rolls in the refrigerator, and the makings for pizza, so I decided to try making them out of the rolls.

"Oil your hands well and press and squeeze the rolls out. They will be the same size as those little pizzas you can buy at the supermarket.

"Each can fix his own, and it's nice to be able to come up with pizza when a group of hungry kids drop in.

"The rolls take very little space in the refrigerator and are quite reasonably priced."

SUCCESSFUL SALADS

One time we asked folks to tell us how they preserved lettuce, got it crisp and crunchy, and kept it from turning rusty-looking on the cut sides, etc., if kept a few days.

Many restaurants said to clean the lettuce by soaking it in salt water, rinsing it, laying paper towels over it, and then topping with a few ice cubes.

Others said to lay paper towels in the bottom of the bowl to catch the drainage, after putting ice cubes under the towel.

Others used terry cloth towels filled with ice cubes, etc., but you can't keep lettuce using any of these methods without the rusty spots forming.

After trying all the suggestions, I think I can top them.

I got to figuring that if I could put a soap-filled scouring pad under water for as long as two weeks . . . and as long as it was completely covered with the water it wouldn't rust . . . then why wouldn't it work for lettuce? It did!

47

How it works: I filled up a plastic container with water, removed the outside leaves of the lettuce, cut the head of lettuce in half with a stainless steel knife, and plunged all the lettuce completely under water. I set this in my refrigerator and forgot it until I was ready to use it.

Next day I removed one half of the lettuce, shook the ice water out, and proceeded from there to cut off as much as I needed for my salad.

Any portion that is left should be plunged back down in that iced water and replaced in the refrigerator for later use.

This will keep at least a week. (I have kept it two weeks as long as I changed the water every five days.)

You have never in your life tasted such crunchy lettuce!

And look at the money we are going to save by not having rust form.

People who do not have plastic containers can cut the top off a big bleach bottle, rinse it well with vinegar, and then use this for a lettuce container.

The heads of lettuce may be quartered for easy insertion into the containers. I do not recommend cuting them any smaller.

If you buy a big head of lettuce wrapped in plastic, and it won't go into your container . . . before removing the plastic cut directly through plastic and all, remove half the head and use the above method.

The remaining portion of plastic may be drawn over the cut half of the head and this put in your hydrator for future use.

There were two schools of thought when it came to breaking lettuce or cutting it up for salads.

Those who said breaking it was the only way, gave no

reason. We found that the heat from our hands sort of wilted the lettuce when compared to cutting it.

One famous chain of restaurants said that they never break lettuce with their hands because it bruises the leaves, removes the crispness, etc. They all suggested sharp, stainless steel knives.

Hotels cut a head in half, turn the cut side down on a cutting board, then slice away, making pieces any size they desire. They use stainless steel spoons to toss it with (never warm hands) so the pieces will separate. This we found to be perfect . . . quick and easy.

And now that I have found the perfect answer, I am going to quit trying different methods and stick to this.

So . . . happy savings with your next head of lettuce (no need to waste a leaf now) and here's for a crisp, crunchy, nondroopy salad . . . without rust.

From Maryland: "To prevent a VEGETABLE SALAD from becoming soggy (if it has to stand awhile) place a saucer upside down on the bottom of the bowl before filling it.

"Until you remove it, the saucer keeps the salad separated from the moisture and it remains fresh and crisp."

From Vermont: "I wonder if you have ever been faced with the problem of head lettuce on sale, but NO FRESH TOMATOES.

"Here is how I solved the problem: I bought a can of good-grade tomatoes and chilled them overnight in the refrigerator, cut them into small pieces, just as I would have done if they had been fresh, and made my salad.

"My family didn't even notice the difference, and the salad was delicious."

GELATIN

Question: Just HOW can I UNMOLD A GELATIN SALAD? Mine tears and looks as if it was never in a mold. I always feel that my efforts are wasted.

Answer: Try greasing your mold with mayonnaise! And never pour your hot gelatin into the mold immediately. Let it cool a bit first. Then the heat won't melt the mayonnaise.

After the gelatin has congealed, turn the container over and run some hot tap water over the back of the mold. It will loosen beautifully. Sometimes, if you have greased it enough, a small TAP on the pan shakes it loose.

If your salad is large, try setting it in a pan of hot water until it loosens. Then dry the bottom of the mold and turn it over on a plate.

"I have always dreaded making gelatin dessert for my family because of the time involved trying to get all the hardened gelatin from around the sides of the bowl.

"Well, I finally found a new and really instant way. . . .

"Instead of pouring the hot water into the bowl of gelatin, I pour the gelatin directly from the box into the pan of boiling water (turn off heat before adding the gelatin.) I stir a few times, and presto, the gelatin dissolves instantly!

This method saves me all the time I used to spend, standing there stirring, and now my family enjoys having gelatin more often."

Well, well, well . . .

Try it, gals. So it takes a little longer for the gelatin to set . . . at least there are no little granules left. I had no idea that one could use TWO cups of hot water since none of the directions said so. The granules dissolve immediately. Most amazing.

Here's another hint when making quick gelatin:

The recipes say to use one cup of boiling water, add ice cubes for three minutes, then "remove those which are not dissolved." No wonder we sometimes come up with supposed-to-be congealed salad that doesn't!

If the water was boiling hot, the ice cubes would melt faster. If the water was from the hot water faucet, then not as much of the ice cubes would melt. Making for thick desserts one day and thin ones the next, etc.

Here's the way I make it when using the quick method:

Use a pint fruit jar. Pour it about half-full of boiling water (No need to measure exactly) then pour in your gelatin and stir with a spoon. Fill the jar with ice cubes. It's GOT to be a perfect two cupfuls! That is what a pint is!

Put the lid on, and from time to time, pick up the jar, give it a quick shake and turn it over when you walk through the kitchen. When it begins to thicken and all the ice has melted, then pour into your mold.

By using this sure measuring method, I get perfectly congealed gelatin every time and only have that one jar to wash.

FOR SAVORY SAUSAGE

A famous pancake house wrote that they always boil their link sausages in water for about 10 minutes, then drain them in a colander. All of the grease which boils out will float on top of the hot water!

After the sausages are cool, they can be put in the refrigerator or freezer until you are ready to use them.

By boiling the sausages 10 to 30 minutes (depending on how much fat they contain), you will find that most of the meat is already cooked, and all it needs then is a slight browning.

We have also been told by restaurateurs that overcooking sausage is what *toughens* it!

And, they recommend that you start sausage in a cold skillet, and cook over a low fire.

In case you are wondering—boiling the fat out does *not* detract from the flavor of sausage. I find it even makes it tastier! I never cook sausage any other way, now.

WONDERS WITH WIENERS

We all have to serve wieners (hot dogs, frankfurters, whatever you call them) once in a while for the budget's sake, but not having much of a yen for them, I have been experimenting with various recipes to make them more to my family's liking.

Now we serve them often, and do you know why?

Well, we ordered wieners in a big restaurant, and they were so delicious (and at the price we paid, they *had* to be good) that I went to their kitchen to learn how they were prepared. Here's how:

They lay thawed wieners (I prepare four at a time) side by side on a piece of foil. With a *sharp* knife, they score all of them at one time, diagonally, about one-eighth-inch deep with about one-fourth-inch between scores. Then, the wieners are turned over and the scoring process is repeated on the other side, resulting in little "diamond" shapes on the wieners. They do not season them.

The foil is then closed. The top and ends are double-folded to keep juices in, and the package is then placed directly in the center of the oven rack in a preheated, 350-degree oven.

After thirty minutes slit open the top of the foil to let a wee bit of steam escape, in order to get a slight browning across the little scores of those nice, juicy wieners.

If you want those "dogs" to be on Cloud Nine, sprinkle them with Parmesan cheese, or paprika, a few minutes before serving. The scores hold the cheese or paprika on the dog.

This is "yummy" when served on a bed of steaming sauerkraut.

Or, how about baking a pot of beans to go along with this? Wow!

From Idaho: "I wanted to serve hot dogs for lunch, but didn't want to light the oven just TO WARM THE WIENER BUNS.

"So, I laid the partly-opened buns (two at a time) lengthwise over the slots on top of the toaster and turned it on. DON'T dare try to push the rolls down into the toaster! Heat from the toaster will go up into the buns and brown them nicely.

"Be sure to turn the toaster on LOW or LIGHT when you use this method, so the wiener rolls will not burn.

"If turned on low, and the buns are not browned to your liking, just repeat the process."

SIMPLIFIED FRYING

If you are one of those darlings who likes fried shrimp, but hates cleaning the fishy oil out of the deep fryer, try frying this type of food DIRECTLY in a two- or three-pound shortening can.

Natch, you have to remove the label from the outside of the can, so it won't catch on fire, but the lid may be left attached to a shortening can, and left open while frying the goodies.

After you have finished frying, all you have to do is let

the oil cool, close the lid, and put the can away for the next time. If you use a coffee can with a plastic lid, just snap it back on the can of cooled grease, and label the top "FISH," so you won't use it for anything else.

This saves washing a pan or deep fryer.

Also, because the can is tall, it keeps spatters off the stove—so we eliminate *that* nasty clean-up job, too.

Never fill the can over one-third full of oil. It will bubble when you put the shrimp in and might boil over. This is good advice for any deep frying.

SPAGHETTI

A woman wrote to us about a new way to cook macaroni and spaghetti, and it seemed unbelievable until we tried it.

Folks, this is absolutely the most terriffc discovery—considering how many pots of macaroni I have overcooked, underboiled and burned. My macaroni was absolutely perfect.

Here is the way we cooked it:

We took two or three quarts of water—(according to how much macaroni you are going to cook)—and brought it to a rolling boil. And, ladies, a rolling boil *means* when the bubbles come to the surface and burst quickly. Put some salt in. Then pour in your macaroni and stir it quickly with a spoon . . . to allow the hot water to touch ALL of the macaroni parts.

Put the top back on your pan, give it a twist, and make sure it is on TIGHT. Then turn off the fire, and allow the lid to REMAIN on the pot of macaroni for 20 minutes. This woman's specific directions were, "Do NOT lift the lid of the pot during these 20 minutes."

Immediately after the 20 minutes are up, remove the

pan from the stove, pour the water off and proceed with your usual recipe. You can pour it into a colander and rinse with cold water if you are cooking it ahead of time. This prevents it from overcooking. It can also be reheated.

As another suggestion: Instead of making just enough for your supper tonight you can make a little bit more and put some of it in a fruit jar and fill it up with cold water and put it into your refrigerator. Tomorrow or the next day this can be used for macaroni salad, casseroles, etc.

This hint can be used for any boxed pasta product. Sure saves lots of pot watching.

FOOD COLORING IN SPAGHETTI

I am so excited I can hardly wait to tell you about this idea. . . .

It's not only for those who are on tight budgets, but also for those who just love spaghetti with meatballs or meat sauce.

The main complaint I have gotten from husbands is, "My wife serves spaghetti, and it's so colorless and unappetizing."

Well, MY husband got to where he said the same thing.

When I was boiling spaghetti one night, after putting salt and a little oil in the water, it dawned on me, "Why can't this look like egg noodles—so rich-looking and yellow?"

So I picked up my bottle of yellow food coloring, and poured in ten drops of the food coloring. After all, I couldn't lose anything but a box of spaghetti if my husband didn't like it. . . .

I could not believe that the coloring would actually soak

into the spaghetti itself, and make it the rich, beautiful color of our homemade egg noodles.

But you know what? It did!

It was the most luscious, egg-colored spaghetti you have ever seen in your life. It looked like it was made from pure butter and eggs.

My husband commented that it looked like it had cheese in it.

So, gals, next time you cook some spaghetti, please put a little bit of yellow food coloring in it. You'll be surprised how appetizing it looks—the psychological effect is most amazing!

This also works with egg noodles, and that plain ol' white macaroni we buy.

Be sure to pick up a little bottle of yellow food coloring. It's one of the least expensive things you can purchase for your household today and it isn't loaded with calories.

LUSCIOUS SPAGHETTI SAUCE

I had a wonderful Italian gentleman cook come into my home to show me how he could cook a special spaghetti sauce that usually takes eight hours in less than forty-five minutes!

Here's how: He put the tomatoes, chopped onions, seasonings, etc. (everything you want in the sauce *except* the meat) in my blender!

He let it run for one minute on high speed. This thoroughly mixed and homogenized all of those delicious condiments into one little thin stream. And don't get discouraged here, gals. It looks white and foamy but settles back to normal within ten minutes of cooking.

One thing he did, which surprised me no end, was to add some bacon grease. I learned that a little bacon grease really adds something.

If you are using meatballs, which he did, make them very, very small instead of the usual two-bite size. All he did was throw them on a foil-lined cookie sheet under the broiler, turning it on high heat.

You know what this did?

The broiler immediately seared the meat, keeping the juices in. And every time he stirred those teensy-weensy balls, they got more beautiful.

The reason for this is that the juice from the hamburger meat gets down on the foil-lined pan, and every time you stir them with a spoon, they get covered with more grease, which seals in more of the flavor.

He broiled the hamburger balls until they were golden brown on all sides. One could do this on the top rack in the oven.

After the spaghetti sauce had been cooking slowly for about forty minutes, he dumped the piping hot, lusciously broiled meatballs into the sauce along with part of the meat drippings, as he said that this would give the sauce that "eight-hour cooking taste."

After letting it simmer for about five minutes, he turned off the fire under the sauce, put a lid on the pot, and let the whole kaboodle stand about ten minutes before serving.

Just as he kept saying, "There is no use cooking something six or eight hours when you can do it in one, is there? Taste this, Heloise . . ."

He was so right. His sauce was out of this world! And it was thick, too.

That fine gentleman from Italy showed me there was

really a cloud TEN! And it takes very little effort to get there!

So instead of wasting six or eight hours cooking spaghetti sauce, why don't you little darlings who have a blender try putting *everything* (except the meat) in it, and make the sauce in forty-five minutes, as he did?

I also learned that if you have no blender, you can use the tiniest holes on your hand grater and grate a potato (leaving the skin on) and a carrot into spaghetti sauce if you want it extremely thick. Besides, it stretches the sauce and adds vitamins. And if you add thin slices of green pepper to the sauce, it makes it out of this world.

Also, when you make spaghetti sauce, clean out your refrigerator at the same time. Use such things as leftover pork, ham, chicken, turkey, sliced tomato left from dinner the night before, etc., and put it all in the blender.

These things are what change the taste of routine spaghetti sauce!

And for your LEFTOVER SPAGHETTI SAUCE, when there's not quite enough for another meal, one woman wrote:

"I fry a pound of hamburger, boil some beans, add the spaghetti sauce and some chili powder, and presto chango, instant chili."

SAUCE CUBES

From Nevada: "When I make spaghetti sauce, I usually triple my recipe, since I also use this same sauce for hot dogs.

"After the sauce cools, I pour it into ice-cube trays and freeze it. Then I remove the cubes and put them into a plastic bag and place in my freezer.

"Now, I can have individual sauce for hot dogs without any trouble."

TOAST THAT IS "THE MOST"

From Wisconsin: "Here's a toasty tip!

"To eliminate most of the crumbs and irregular halves from a slice of TOAST, cut a 'Dutch dart' in the bread before toasting. Cut bread diagonally from corner to corner but not through the crust.

"Result: Only the crust needs to be broken when the toast pops up."

Don't throw away that LEFTOVER PIECE OF TOAST after breakfast. Save it.

Either put it in your freezer or back in your oven with the pilot light still on and let it get real dried out and crisp.

Next time you make a lettuce salad, cut the piece of toast in small cubes. Just before you sit down to eat, add the cubes on top of your salad. Great.

Makes the salad go further and gives it a completely different taste with BODY, especially if you have sprinkled the toast with Parmesan cheese or a little garlic salt.

Always toss the salad *before* sprinkling the toast tidbits on top.

THIN TOASTED SANDWICH

"For THIN toasted sandwiches, toast a slice of bread in your toaster and then slice it THROUGH the edge with a serrated knife. The firm toasted surface guides the knife for easy cutting.

"Butter the untoasted surfaces and fill for a dainty, crisp sandwich."

Honeychile, this is the hottest hint to head our way in many a moon!

We tried it on three different kinds of bread, and it worked beautifully on all three.

What a boon this will be for weight-watchers—who STARVE for a closed sandwich, and yet must always eat them open-faced style!

The same holds true for a poached or coddled egg that just doesn't taste so good without toast under it.

And, too, some people love the taste of toasted sandwiches. This way you have toast on the outside, but soft, moist bread next to the filling . . . which will hold the spreads, etc.

It is absolutely amazing the way a serrated knife will cut through a piece of toast while it is still warm.

So those of you who are on diets—shift gears with me right now—and start slicing that slice of toast in half.

See how wonderful it is. Just lay toast flat on cutting board when slicing. This will leave you with two very thin pieces of toast.

If you don't put anything on it but a thinly sliced tomato, a piece of lettuce, and a sliced hard-boiled egg—at least you FEEL like you have eaten a real sandwich but have eaten only half as much bread!

And for those of you who feel that you cannot afford the luxury of mayonnaise, yet don't like mustard . . . try squirting some juice from a fresh lemon or lime on the lettuce! Great.

TOAST

Don't get into the habit of buying one kind of bread all the time. Buy white, brown and raisin once in a while. Open each package and mix 'em up every three or four pieces. (Reseal and freeze the rest.)

Be surprised how you will enjoy reaching for a piece of bread to find a variety every few slices. Too, it makes a change in breakfast and the kiddies love it.

And remember for a variation on cinnamon toast you can mix instant coffee with sugar and have coffee toast. Great.

Orange toast too. Try mixing granulated orange drinks with sugar. Scrump-tily-umptious!

FREEZER EASYS

From Arizona: "Whenever I have the time, I beat up a whole box of whipped topping mix (looks like whipped cream, but has fewer calories). I drop blobs of it on a waxed paper-lined cookie sheet, and freeze the whole lot.

"When solidly frozen, I remove and put them in a plastic bag and return to the freezer.

"The great thing about making up the whole box at one time is that when I am in a hurry, these FROZEN DABS OF WHIPPED TOPPING can be removed (as many or as few as I need), and placed on top of gelatin desserts, puddings, ice cream sundaes, pound cake or canned fruits. I even use them on hot apple or cherry pies.

"By making up the whole box at once, I have to wash a bowl only once, and the topping is always ready whenever I need it."

From Texas: "For EXTRA-LARGE AND DIFFERENT ICE CUBES, I use cupcake tins. Just fill the trays with water and freeze!

"To thaw, I run a little water over the bottom of the pan and the cubes slip free!

"'These large cubes are wonderful for punch bowls."

From California: "I save all the STEAK JUICES, and put them in a container in the freezer; then, when I have a roast of beef, I use the juice along with the roast gravy.

"Yummy! Plus, it gives me more gravy, as there never seems to be enough."

If you have A PITCHER OF JUICE, or some other drink which you want to chill without "watering it down," put your ice cubes in a plastic bag, close the end of the bag with a rubber band, and put the bag and all in the pitcher of juice.

REFRIGERATOR TRICKS

Did you know that BREADING will cling to pork chops, chicken, eggplant, etc., much better if the item is coated and put in the refrigerator for a few hours before frying? 'Tis true. Try it.

From Louisiana: "Here is one for people who like fish.

"Put the fish in a tray of water and freeze it. When it is frozen remove the fish (in the block of ice) from the pan and wrap.

"When you get ready to cook the fish, just defrost the water and the fish at the same time."

Many people write that they do this. But be sure to clean the fish first! And let's hope it's a big one!

REFRIGERATOR TRADE

From New Jersey: "Our next-door neighbors have no children, and neither have we.

"Both of us gals love to cook and bake, but were always faced with THE PROBLEM OF LEFTOVERS (no deepfreezers), until we came up with the idea of swapping them!

"When she cooks a kettle of ham and beans, vegetable soup, etc., she brings me whatever is left over from their dinner. If I bake a pie, make a gelatin salad or such, I take part of it to her.

"This way, neither family feels it is eating leftovers."

MIXED-UP LEFTOVERS

For those of you who eat GRAVY every day like we do, have you ever tried using leftover coffee instead of milk or water?

If not, why not? It's really great. Sure changes the taste of the usual old gravy.

From New York: "I made the most delicious rice pudding with my LEFTOVER EGGNOG, using the eggnog mix in place of the milk. I added plenty of raisins and a little cinnamon.

"Formerly I discarded the eggnog that remained at the end of a holiday."

That's a delicious idea! I usually put my leftover eggnog in a milk carton and put it in the freezer until some later time when eggnog appeals to us. Also, I sometimes just whack the frozen carton on concrete steps a few times to break up the frozen nog, and put some chunks of it in sweet milk for drinking.

From Indiana: "We love white cakes and angel food cakes at our house, but I always had the problem of what to do with the leftover egg yolks.

"My next-door neighbor solved this for me. Now I poach the yolks until they are firm, let them cool, then put them through my sieve.

"They are wonderful for garnishing soups, salads and appetizers."

FOOD SAVERS

From West Virginia: "For those who buy HONEY IN JARS and find it turning to sugar, I suggest that they put the jar in a warm oven with the lid off, and let it heat slowly. The crystallization will disappear."

Thank you! I had never tried putting the jar in the oven at a low temperature. I always had put it in a pan of water, brought the water to a boil, shut off the fire and let it set. This usually did the trick for me, but then I was using an extra pan for nothing, eh?

When butter becomes stale, put it in a bowl, set it on the drainboard and let it come to room temperature. Pour it in your mixer, add a dab of milk and beat it well. Drain off the excess milk. The milk absorbs the rancidness of the butter and it will be fluffy and fresh again.

ADDITIONS THAT COUNT
From South Carolina: "My boys used to turn up their noses at soups because they were watery. One day I sprinkled some instant potato flakes in the soup. They just loved this THICK SOUP."

From Connecticut: "I put five or six marshmallows on top of COCOA when heating and stirring, and they prevent scum from forming on the top.

"I also put a marshmallow in a vacuum bottle before pouring in the hot chocolate mixture. Saves sugar, too, since the marshmallows are sweet."

Did you know that when making CHICKEN OR TURKEY DRESSING and the eggs are a pale color, you can add a few drops of yellow food coloring and the result will be the most tempting-looking golden-yellow dressing? I also add a few drops of this yellow coloring to giblet gravy.

SWEET 'N' SOUR
From New Jersey: "Since so many people are using SACCHARIN, it would be most helpful for them to know how to melt a tablet.

"Put a saccharin tablet in a teaspoon, squeeze in a drop or two of fresh lemon juice, and the tablet will melt instantly! This eliminates trying to mash it in the bottom of a glass."

From Idaho: "If just a few drops of LEMON JUICE are required in a recipe, puncture a lemon on one end with a knife and squeeze out the required amount of juice. The rest of the lemon will keep until it is needed."

MORE FLAVORSOME BREAKFASTS

From Oklahoma: "For those who love OATMEAL, I wonder if they have ever tried putting chocolate syrup on it! Sure is different and makes it so tasty.

"We sometimes shake cinnamon in the water before boiling the oats. This is good, too.

"And one morning my son put vanilla in the oats and gave it a quick stir just before removing it from the fire.

"Our whole family loved that."

On pancake day, when you run out of SYRUP, try adding a little water and a dab of butter to some fruit jelly, and heat. It makes a delicious fruit syrup, and there's plenty for all.

CAN DO!

If you buy cans of ham—or ham in cans—whichever way it is makes no matter, eh? As long as we can find a way to save on our budget, and KEEP THE HAMS FROM DRYING OUT.

I found a way to do this.

After opening the can, throw away the cut-off top, but save the bottom. Do not rinse or scald it.

Cut off as much of the ham as you need, and put the remaining portion on a plate and turn the empty can UPSIDE DOWN over it.

No matter what shape the ham is, it will fit inside the can and will remain fresh and moist when put back into the refrigerator.

How simple can life be? I have tried this over and over again, and it works like a charm.

This can also be used for other things that come in cans

such as lunch meats, tomato aspic, cranberry sauce, potted sandwich spreads, Vienna sausages, corned beef, dog foods, etc.

From Rhode Island: "To keep your SHORTENING FRESH, open the can with a mechanical opener (this leaves smooth edges) and cover with the plastic lid from a coffee can of the same size. It will fit perfectly.

"When using this method, do NOT open the shortening can with attached key. When you do, you remove the lip necessary to keep the plastic lid on tight."

"Turn a can of soup, vegetables (or anything that might settle to the bottom of the can) UPSIDE DOWN BEFORE OPENING with a can opener.

"It is so much easier to have the contents pour out instead of having to scrape around in the bottom of the can to get the last bean or all of the soup from the bottom."

THAT PRECIOUS PRESSURE COOKER

From Kentucky: "For those who have PRESSURE COOKERS:

"Wrap different vegetables separately and loosely in foil, then cook. Turn the little individual heavy foil containers up around the edges to form sort of a bowl so that the water does not get into the vegetables. Just place these on top of the grate in your pressure cooker. You save all the vitamins, and the vegetables have a wonderful flavor.

"Put what is left over into the refrigerator in the same

piece of foil and warm it the next day. Even warmed-over potatoes are real good this way."

That's great! I just tried cut carrots in one foil container, potato wedges in another and fresh green beans in a third. I rolled the vegetables in the foil as if I were going to bake a potato, then took a knife and cut an "X" in the top, folding the top gently back to allow for cooking, and punched a hole in the bottom of the foil.

EQUIPMENT CARE PAYS OFF

Here's a hint for women lucky enough to have a GARBAGE DISPOSAL: After grinding anything that causes odors in your kitchen, such as onions or fish, drop a slice of lemon, orange or grapefruit peel into the disposal.

The pleasant fragrance of the rind wipes away any possibility of problems.

From Ohio: "After making milk shakes in our ELECTRIC BLENDER, the milk always left a coating after the blender was rinsed out.

"Now all I do is add two cups of water, a few drops of dish-washing liquid, and turn on the blender.

"After a few seconds I dump the water out, rinse out the soap and I have a shiny, clean blender."

From Alaska: "When the COFFEE BASKET IN YOUR PERCOLATOR GETS PLUGGED with coffee grounds, just set it over the simmer burner or pilot light on your stove.

"When the basket gets hot and dry, just tap it and the coffee grounds will fall out!"

It works! But I caution you on one thing—do not let the basket get red-hot. Pick up the stem (that's the long narrow gadget on the end) with a hot pad, and tap it

easily. Never, never let it get too hot. All we want to do is dry it out. And all these years I've tried to pick the grounds out with a toothpick!

MELLOW CUTTING BOARD

From Arkansas: "I have a small but useful hint for keeping a CUTTING BOARD attractive.

"When my board was new, I rubbed cooking oil on it to season it and give it a mellow finish. Now, after using it every few times, I wash and dry the board, then rub cooking oil on it to subdue the knife cuts.

"If you will notice, the cutting boards in meat markets always have a mellow look . . . caused by the fat on the meat."

TRIO OF TIMESAVERS

From Iowa: "I would like to tell you of one more use I have found for that indispensable nylon net.

"Being a farm wife, I raise and DRESS MY OWN BROILERS. After the chicken is killed and the feathers plucked, I take a piece of nylon net (kept especially for this purpose) and rub the chicken all over with this to remove that thin layer of yellow skin which sometimes takes so much time and scraping to get off.

"I just put the chicken in a pan of water, or hold it

under a faucet of running water, and scrub it with the net. The yellow skin comes off like magic.

"When finished, wash the net out under hot water, take it outside and shake out the remaining particles. Hang up to dry, and it will be ready to use again."

From Idaho: "When I want TO SOFTEN BUTTER quickly for spreading, I fill a bowl with boiling water, then pour out the water and turn the hot bowl upside down over the butter dish.

"The butter will soften without melting, and is great for corn on the cob, buttering French bread, etc."

From South Carolina: "I always keep a large shaker of SALT MIXED WITH A SMALL AMOUNT OF PEPPER in the kitchen.

"Most foods which require salt also require pepper, so this two-in-one method has two advantages:

"First, instead of having to pick up two shakers to season the 'vittles,' I pick up only one. Multiply how many times you pick up that kitchen salt shaker, and you can visualize how many hours you will save in your lifetime.

"Secondly, I'm a little absentminded, and sometimes forget whether or not I have salted something! I can just glance at the food, and if I see any grains of pepper, I know it has also been salted!"

CHEERS FOR ALUMINUM FOIL

From Pennsylvania: "In the kitchen, aluminum foil is my best friend. It's disposable, and to me worth every penny for time and effort saved.

"I never use a plain COOKIE SHEET; instead, I put a

sheet of foil over the cold oven shelf when I start to bake cookies or biscuits, and then put the shelf back in the oven. Saves pans.

"Haven't used a PAN LID for a long time. I mold a tight cover of foil over the pan. When necessary, I use a fork to punch holes in the foil so the steam can escape. No boil-over results, and most of the nutritional values are saved as well. This is especially useful when you have a pot which has no lid to fit."

"When I make grilled cheese sandwiches on my electric grill, I first lay a piece of FOIL ON THE GRILL, put the sandwiches on the foil, cover them with another piece of foil, and close the top.

"This is easier than cleaning up the cheese that usually oozes out."

And you know what? For those who don't have electric sandwich grills, the foil can be put in the bottom of an iron skillet!

From New Hampshire: "Save and wash your empty ALUMINUM FROZEN-DINNER TRAYS to bake buns and rolls for freezing. You will be surprised how many buns the trays will hold.

"After baking the rolls, I cool them on racks, then put them back into the small trays and cover them with foil. They are ready for freezing and for reheating later."

Puncture holes in the bottom of an aluminum foil pie pan and use this as a LID FOR SPAGHETTI SAUCE OR SOUP. It lets the steam out, keeps the sauce or soup from becoming watery, and prevents the usual splashes and splatters from getting all over the stove.

KITCHEN GADGETRY

When you use a POTATO PEELER to clean carrots, always hold the small end of the carrot with your fingers first and peel *toward* the largest end. Then it is much easier to peel the smaller end of the carrot, and there is less chance of nicked fingers.

From New Mexico: "When heating vegetables or making gravies, sauces, or anything that calls for close attention, you have to stir and lay the spoon aside or it will sneak down into the pan the minute you turn your head!

"I solved this problem by bending the handle end of a tablespoon (stainless steel is easiest) so that it will hook over the rim of the pan. Now the stirring spoon is always there when I turn back."

"If you use a serrated grapefruit spoon TO SCOOP OUT THE PULP OF TOMATOES, it is much quicker, and the tomatoes will have a neater appearance. Makes a lovely tomato cup for those salads."

This has all the other methods beat by a country mile! When you use a knife to do this, the tomatoes usually come out jagged, or you cut through them, and they aren't nearly as even and eye-appealing when stuffed with tuna salad, shrimp salad or what-have-you.

From Hawaii: "Have you ever had a pan of food cooking and found the STEAM ESCAPING and your stove in a mess?

"Try putting a toothpick between the lid and the pan and this will let the steam out a little at a time. Thus no messy stove to clean!"

From South Dakota: "I heard about using a piece of sponge for PADDING THE FAUCET to prevent broken dishes.

"I had the same trouble so I took a white rubber caster (such as we use on chair legs to protect floors), cut the thick bottom part off the caster and slipped the ring part on the end of the faucet. Works fine."

VACUUM THOUGHTS

From Wisconsin: "Did you ever look into your VACUUM BOTTLE and see the small brown film left from coffee?

"To remove this film, tear up some newspaper into small pieces, put it in the vacuum bottle, add a small amount of detergent and hot water, soak a few minutes; then shake and wash.

"Presto! You have a bright, shiny vacuum bottle."

From Kentucky: "When on trips, I take my VACUUM BOTTLE into a restaurant to be filled with hot coffee.

"I always had trouble getting the cork to stay in while the coffee was still hot, until a waitress told me to roll the cork in sugar before inserting it in the bottle. This really works. The cork stays in and the coffee stays hot."

WOULD-YOU-BELIEVE-IT KITCHEN TRICKS

From Georgia: "Even with the modern kitchen equipment, I still like to use my HAND BEATER occasionally. But,

73

as you know, beating anything in a bowl will cause splashes.

"I solved this problem by taking a plastic bowl cover large enough to fit over the bowl, making a hole in the center, and inserting the beater. The elastic around the edge of the cover keeps it in place on the bowl and you can beat away with no more splashes."

Know what? This also works with an electric beater! Just make the hole oblong and larger. Lots easier to wash the cover than the wall.

From a man in Indiana: "This may sound laughable but it truly works. About once a year, I use a blowtorch to remove any accumulation from my wife's cast iron skillets and kettles.

"For those who do not have blowtorches, are they aware that any garage could do this for them?"

Ever notice how the members of your family hang around the kitchen while you are doing your baking? They certainly take a very keen interest, and are never far away when it comes time to lick the frosting or wolf down the tarts you make from leftover crust. Well, here are some tips so you'll never disappoint 'em.

SMART COOKIES
From Georgia: "This hint is a surprise for those little cookie eaters, as well as a great time-saver:

"When CUTTING OUT COOKIES, leave enough space between each cookie for fantastically shaped ones with all the odd pieces of dough that are left.

"Grandma's 'crazy cookies' are the favorites in our home."

From New York: "Each time you bake cookies, squares, etc., freeze a few.

"In no time you'll have a real assortment of goodies put away.

"When unexpected guests arrive (and they aren't watching) dive for your supply of FROZEN COOKIES, and they will thaw in no time.

"Your guests will marvel at your fare!"

FOR PRIZE-WINNING PIES

From Alaska: "Want to keep the JUICE IN THE PIE instead of in the oven?

"Make your top crust large and put it on loose, pushing it back toward the center of the pie. Then seal the edges as usual. The loose crust will expand with the steam, and the juice will remain in the pie."

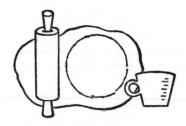

You can also cut a few slits in the center to let steam escape—according to what kind of pie you are baking—but the wrinkles in the top do work.

From Michigan: "Here is the recipe for an easy CHOCO-LATE-BOTTOM PIE.

"After baking the shell (or you could use the crumbly-type shell), just take a broken-up chocolate bar or some chocolate chips and sprinkle them on the pie shell. Cover this with hot custard or vanilla pudding.

"The hot pudding will melt the chocolate, thus making the chocolate-bottom part of the pie.

"I always shave some more of the candy bar on top of meringue. This is very pretty when done with a vegetable peeler. It adds that extra something to the pie."

ONE PAN, TWO PIES

From New York: "When TWO DIFFERENT FRUIT FILL-INGS are desired, put a circle of pastry in a twelve-inch pie pan. Put filling in half of it and fold the other half of the dough over to the outer edge of the pan and crimp the edges together. This will look like a fried pie.

"Roll out another circle of pastry, fit it in the same pan with the wide part against the other pie and pour in the other filling.

"Fold over the top half to the other outer edge of the pan, and seal. Cut steam vents in each section, and bake as usual.

"I have found this to be a great time-saver, especially on busy days."

From California: "Here is a delicious idea for using LEFTOVER PIE CRUST.

"Roll out your leftover pie dough and spread lightly with margarine or butter. Then sprinkle some brown sugar all over it and roll it up! Slice into little rolls about one inch wide and bake until golden brown.

"We always looked for these roly-polys on Mother's baking day!"

SLICE A NICE CAKE

From Ohio: "I ordered A LARGE CAKE for my father's birthday. It was so big that I knew if I tried to cut it with a knife, I would have a mess.

"So I took a length of regular sewing thread and doubled it, and then pulled it down through the center of the cake, cutting it in half. Then I used the thread again to cut the cake in quarters.

"After that I could cut the cake easily with a knife."

From Ohio: "I have been bothered at times by cakes that come out of the pan TOO CRUMBLY. When I attempt to ice them, either the icing lumps or the crumbs stick to the icing knife.

"A very simple remedy, if one has sufficient freezer space, is to put the cake into the freezer until it is firm, then ice the cake. The frosting goes on smoothly, the crumbs stay in place, and no one ever knows it wasn't a perfect cake."

FROSTING DELIGHTS

For a quick and delicious cupcake (or cake) ICING, melted marshmallows are the greatest!

Just a few minutes before removing cupcakes from the oven, top each one with a marshmallow, and they will melt to cover the cakes with yummy frosting. Don't leave 'em too long—just until melted and slightly brown. Delish!

When baking loaf cake or making TEA CAKES in your muffin tins, do you know that you can break up a milk chocolate bar, and the minute you take your cakes from the oven, lay a square of chocolate on the top of each *hot* tea cake (or if you're making loaf cake, break it up in pieces and spread them out), let it melt, then take your knife, give the chocolate a few swirls and you've saved yourself the job of making icing. What's more, there is no bowl to wash!

'Cause the cake is hot, the candy bar will melt, so spread it over the cake as soon as it melts. If you don't get around to spreading the melted candy over the cake, no matter; you will have *some* icing on your cake with little effort on your part.

From California: "This little tip on frosting is very tasty. If you have ever tasted peanut butter cups, you will know what a treat this is.

"When making CHOCOLATE FROSTING, add about a table-spoon of peanut butter. This not only tastes yummy, but it gives the frosting a creamy consistency."

PARTY CAKE CANDLE HOLDERS

"Would mothers like to make their own birthday-candle holders for their children's birthday cakes? I make the kind which can also be eaten.

"I dip pitted MARASCHINO CHERRIES into heavy syrup and then into finely chopped nuts. The cherries also can be rolled in powdered sugar. These make perfect birthday-candle holders.

"Put the cherry on top of the cake and stick the tiny candle in the hole of the cherry!"

"MINIATURE MARSHMALLOWS make very pretty holders for candles on a child's birthday cake.

"And do you know that they protect the frosting from the melting candle wax?"

"I was baking a birthday cake for my six-year-old son when I noticed I had failed to buy candle holders.

"I had some GUMDROPS on hand, so decided to use these instead, using a kitchen implement to make a hole for the candle.

"This went over big with my children, and the colors were beautiful."

WRITE IT DOWN

From Michigan: "I love to cook, and trying new recipes is one of my favorite pastimes, but I have so many cookbooks that I could never remember which recipe was in which book.

"It finally occurred to me to tape a large sheet of paper inside the door of the cabinet where I keep the recipe books.

"When I try a recipe, and know I'll want to use it again, I just write down the name of the recipe, the cookbook, and the page number on which it appears.

"When I want to make almond chicken, Hungarian goulash, or what have you, I just glance at the recipe list, and reach for the right cookbook.

"No more looking through half a dozen or more books to find the recipe I want."

79

It helps to fasten a MENU NOTE to the refrigerator door when you are giving a party, so relishes or the like don't get overlooked.

Also, a dire warning fastened to the door might prevent refrigerator-raiders from helping themselves beforehand!

FIRE DO'S AND DON'TS

Don't—I repeat—don't use flour and cornstarch TO EXTINGUISH GREASE FIRES.

It's dangerous and here's a letter from a fire inspector explaining why:

"Flour and cornstarch are combustible materials and when they are suspended in the air, so that they mix readily with the oxygen in the air, they burn very rapidly; in fact, they may cause an explosion.

"Salt is an old-time remedy for fighting a kitchen fire. Salt does no harm but it doesn't do much good either.

"The best extinguishing agent in the kitchen is baking soda. When thrown on a fire, it produces carbon dioxide gas which excludes the oxygen and extinguishes the fire.

"The extinguishers approved for use on flammable liquid and electrical fires contain either bicarbonate of soda or carbon dioxide. It's a good idea to have one of these extinguishers handy in the kitchen.

"If you don't have an extinguisher, use the box of baking soda."

THE TRUTH ABOUT CONVENIENCE FOODS

Do you ever have a guilty feeling about buying "CONVENIENCE FOODS" instead of starting from scratch to prepare a certain dish?

Well, don't!

According to the U.S. Department of Agriculture: For

each $100.00 spent for food in a grocery store, about $12.55 goes for convenience foods. This same amount of food, in its natural form, would cost $12.82!

How about that?

Ready to Wear

Here's the real secret to the role of household "wardrobe mistress." Do it with love, and it actually becomes a pleasure. Fight it and there's no worse drudgery.

Your first requirement in keeping up the family wardrobe is a sewing machine at the ready and in good working order. If you don't have one, save like mad until you can buy one.

A daughter in the family should learn to take on her own sewing chores as soon as she is old enough. This will relieve you, at the same time it teaches her.

These hints are passed along in hopes of making clothing management a labor of love. There are time-savers as well as ideas for making clothes live longer and look better.

TAME THOSE SHIRTTAILS

From Louisiana: "I had a BLOUSE which was so short it kept pulling out of my skirt. So I sewed a four-inch strip of nylon net around the bottom of the blouse and now have no trouble keeping it in place. The net is not bulky and clings well."

"BLOUSES can be so bulky around the bottom seam if worn inside a skirt.

"I cut off the bottom hem with pinking shears, and the blouse doesn't show a seam around the stomach or hips."

From California: "When little girls' BLOUSES get too short to tuck in, but the shoulders still fit, I buy a yard of printed material and sew a full skirt (with a set-in belt) onto the blouse.

"I add a sash from each side seam of the skirt material, and it makes a darling little dress."

And as everyone knows, the hardest part of making a dress is the top, certainly not the skirt. Try it, gals. It works, and saves on the clothes budget.

"Run, don't walk, to your nearest dime store and buy a yard of rubberized skirt belting if your husband has a problem keeping his no-iron SHIRTS tucked in.

"Cut this strip of belting to fit the waistband in the *back* of the trousers (you'll probably have enough for three pairs) and sew it to the inside of the waistband, from side seam to side seam.

"This should be sewn so that the stitches won't show on the outside of the trousers."

NO MORE BLUE JEANS BLUES

From Virginia: "I reinforce the knees of my children's BLUE JEANS (as soon as they have been through the wash a few times) with iron-on knee patches applied to the inside of the blue jeans.

"I wait until the blue jeans have been washed a few times because it is easier to find the knees. Don't laugh! When I tried putting the patches inside brand-new jeans, I always seemed to get them too high or too low, which defeated my purpose.

"I also fix my husband's denim or cotton work pants the same way. It really saves on the number of knees worn through.

"One can use this idea for other heavy wear spots—the inside of elbows in work shirts, say—*before* the damage is done."

To those of you who have small ones who wear BLUE JEANS to school and the knees of the jeans get white (and some kids just don't like white, faded knees), try getting an all-purpose dye at the drug, dime or department store, mix it in a spray bottle with some hot water, shake it until completely dissolved, and spray on the white part of the jean knees.

It works!

I sprayed some with a rather strong dye (using much less water than it called for), put them out in the sun to dry, and then ironed them with a hot iron. It surely made a difference!

Another way to do this if you have no plunger-type spray bottle: Go to your dime store, buy some crayons and use the blue crayon to rub *gently* back and forth across the fibers of the material. This is especially useful when letting down blue jeans (if you bought them too long and hemmed them up, so they could be worn for a longer period of time) and they have a white line you don't want seen.

After rubbing gently with the dark blue crayon, take your medium-warm iron and iron over the crayon-marked parts. This will melt the colored crayon; it will absorb into the fibers and the white line won't show.

From Virginia: "Do your boys have an old pair of BLUE JEANS that are still good, but faded? Don't throw them away. They are still wearable, and can be darkened so that they will look almost like new.

"Simply drop them in the washer with a pair of new blue jeans that you are shrinking before they are worn. Some dye will come out of the new jeans and cling to the faded ones.

"Result? Two pairs of good-looking jeans."

From New Jersey: "I am the mother of several small boys and they all wear BLUE JEANS.

"Instead of running to the dime store or searching for patches for their blue jeans, I remove one of the many pockets (usually the back), and cut it to the size needed. This makes a wonderful patch that is both economical and a perfect match in color with the faded blue jeans.

"The boys never miss that extra pocket and there is usually a piece left over for the next mending job."

KEEP STRETCHABLES SLEEK

If you want to wear SLACKS with boots, the boots may push the slacks up unless the slacks have straps underfoot.

For those slacks without straps, cut pieces of narrow elastic, buttonhole stitch over the ends of elastic and form a loop (threads back and forth and then buttonhole stitch over loop).

Sew buttons on both seams inside of both pants legs, and attach the buttonholed loops to the buttons.

By putting buttons on your other slacks you can use the same piece of elastic with all.

From Maine: "Did you know that the stretch headbands girls wear make wonderful straps for the bottom of STRETCH PANTS?

"Cut one headband into two pieces, and sew one piece on the bottom of each stretch pants leg."

PAJAMA GAME

From Connecticut: "When making children's flannel PAJAMAS with feet attached, I find iron-on tape (or patches ironed on the bottom of the foot of the pajamas) keeps the feet from wearing as fast, and keeps them cleaner."

And why not press patches of iron-on tape on the bottom of the feet of ready-made pajamas, and make them last longer, too? Great idea, eh?

From West Virginia: "When I buy PAJAMAS with feet in them for my children, invariably the legs are too long and my children walk on the leg part of the pajamas and not on the *feet*.

"Now I have learned to turn the pajamas inside out and take a small hem or tuck around each leg just below the knee. Then I turn the pajamas right side out. Now there are no more dirty pajama legs.

"When the child grows, just rip out the stitching and he can wear the pajamas another year."

From Georgia: "When I make my children's PAJAMAS, I use the cuffs of worn-out socks and sew them on the bottom of the sleeves and legs. The children love their pajamas fixed this way because the legs of the pajamas don't scoot up when they go to bed. Some of the boys' socks have such heavy ribbed cuffs that the cuffs easily outwear the material from which I make the pajamas."

"My husband has a wonderful idea for the fast-growing small child.

"Any mother can make BERMUDAS AND T-TOP SLEEPERS for the summer out of children's winter pajamas, simply by cutting off the arms and legs.

"These are especially useful in an air-conditioned home."

SHOE GROOMING

From Pennsylvania: "For children's WHITE SHOES (which always leave marks on Daddy's suit and everything else they touch): after cleaning them with white polish, let dry, then polish with clean wax paper.

"This leaves a beautiful, hard finish that won't come off, and you'll find they stay clean longer, too."

From Kansas: "Furniture wax sprayed on today's STACK HEELS gives instant beauty and protection against scratches."

From New York: "When the childrens' rubber OVER-SHOES AND GALOSHES have been handed down as many times as ours, they remain dull and dirty-looking even when washed.

"I have found that polishing them with vegetable shortening and a facial tissue (just as you do for black patent-leather shoes) will make them look like new!"

Get rid of SHOE ODORS: The first thing to do is keep your hose or socks clean. Many men's socks have an accumulation of soap in them which some housewives do not rinse out thoroughly. So next time rinse them in a vinegar and water solution.

The odor in hose, socks and shoes is caused primarily by perspiration bacteria. I suggest that as soon as you remove your shoes (especially if they are damp) you crumple up some newspaper and stuff it down into the toes of the shoes. This will absorb some of the moisture that has accumulated in them during the day.

Leave the newspaper in the shoes until you are ready to wear them next time. This will also help to keep their shape.

There are of course foot-deodorant sprays on the market to help combat this problem.

Lots of people who stand on their feet all day buy shoes a size larger and wear removable innersoles which they change often.

From Florida: "When buying white shoes with LACES, I buy an extra pair of laces. When my shoes need polishing, I always have a fresh pair of laces to put in the shoes without waiting for the other pair to dry."

From a teen-ager: "Some of us cut off the sleeves of our sweatshirts above the elbow.

"Instead of discarding the cut-off part, we turn it inside out and sew across the cut end of it.

"You can use these CUT SLEEVES to slip over your best shoes to keep them from being scuffed in the closet.

"When you want to wear the shoes, the sleeve can also be used for a quick buffing. My shoes have never looked so good.

From Georgia: "I have the most fantastic idea for CLEANING SUEDE shoes or anything made of suede: It just happened that one of my old nylon stockings was lying around the other day and I brushed my shoes with it. The results were amazing.

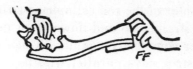

"So I tried brushing everything I have made of suede, such as handbags, belts, etc., and they all look like new, even though some of them are over a year old.

"Now I keep an old stocking handy for just this purpose."

And while we're talking about shoes, one woman wrote me:

"A shoe salesman gave me the following tips on buying shoes:

"It is better to shop for shoes late in the day because feet *spread* as the day goes on (especially during hot weather). Shoes bought early in the morning may be real "pinchers" after you have been on your feet several hours.

"Also, one foot is often slightly larger than the other, so it is wise to buy your shoes to fit the larger foot. Then, buy a pair of innersoles and insert one in the shoe for the smaller foot."

SPEED STITCHERY

"Here is a wonderful idea for SEWING MACHINES:

"Take the *red* strip from a package of cigarettes and a piece of cellophane tape a little longer than the strip. Place the red strip carefully down the center of the sticky side of the tape.

"Measure five-eighths of an inch (the usual seam allowance when sewing) to the right of the hole your sewing-machine needle goes into.

"Lay the center of the red cellophane strip on this mark and extend it straight up and down from this point.

"Then cover completely again with more tape, making sure that the strip stays parallel with the side of the machine all the way.

"Do this very carefully and the little strip will stay on your machine for years."

LOOK MA, NO THREAD!

From Colorado: "I use my sewing machine with a LARGE NEEDLE and no thread to sew around scarves to be finished with a crocheted edge.

"The small crochet needle slips right into the little holes made by the big needle of the sewing machine. Very neat trick."

From Virginia: "If you have one of those new sewing machines that make FANCY STITCHES: After pressing the hem on the dress open, fancy-stitch across that revealing

90

white line. Then put a row of this fancy stitching around the collars and cuffs of the dress, thus making it look adorable.

"No one will ever know that your hem has been let down. Be sure to set your machine on a larger stitch. It makes the prettiest design."

BUTTON TECHNIQUE

Cut MATCHING BUTTONS from old garments and store them between two strips of cellophane tape. The buttons can be seen at a glance, and individual buttons can be snipped from the strip as needed.

Certainly does keep the sewing basket and button box neat! And no time lost searching for one matching button.

When COVERING BUTTONS, and the material is on the sheer side, try cutting a small circle of mending tape and pressing it onto the cover of the button. No metal shows and the buttons last longer.

SEW 'EM ON TO STAY

"For BUTTONS THAT POP OFF at the waistband on shorts, slacks and skirts: Remove the button and sew it on a small piece of elastic, then sew the ends of the elastic to the waistband where you removed the button.

"This gives a bit of leeway; the button can move as you breathe, or gain or lose weight."

Have you ever tried using dental floss instead of thread to sew on those COLLAR BUTTONS your husband so easily twists off his shirts? They will never come off again.

From Pennsylvania: "When SEWING BUTTONS on sweaters, don't knot the thread and sew as usual.

"Leave about three inches of thread on the back when you start, and hold it while you sew the button on, then go through to the back and cut off your thread the same length as the thread you left before. Tie these threads together, and cut. Buttons will stay on much longer."

From Montreal: "When SEWING ON BUTTONS, I always quadruple my thread rather than just double it. The buttons go on faster because I need half the number of stitches to hold them on securely."

From Maine: "Use elastic thread for SEWING HEAVY BUTTONS on coats. The buttons are more secure and it eliminates time spent re-sewing loose buttons. (Or buying new ones.) Elastic thread is sold in dime stores, at department store sewing notions counters, and needlework shops."

From Virginia: "I used to have trouble with the BUTTONS ON MY DUSTERS. They would always be pulling off and tearing the material.

"The last time I bought a duster, I removed the buttons and sewed them on over the buttonholes, tacking the buttonhole beneath.

"Then I put sew-on snaps on the back facing under the buttons, and the other facing.

"My duster is such a joy to wear, and when I pick up my little ones no buttons are pulled off.

"Also, it is easier to take the duster off when in a hurry to start my busy day."

From Wisconsin: "When SEWING BUTTONS ON HEAVY MATERIAL, place a fine-toothed comb between the button and the material.

"The needle goes between the teeth of the comb.

"This is a good way to keep the thread equal for each stitch, and the buttons will not be sewn on too tightly."

BLENDED THREAD

"When mending a garment of more than one color (such as olive and brown), try using TWO THREADS—one of each color—when threading your needle. The two will blend into the material better than if you had used only one."

EASY WIND-UP

"When taking the hem from a dress which you have bought, and you wish to use the same thread to replace the hem, WIND THE THREAD around the neck of a bottle, dampen it and let dry, then use. Will prevent knotting and snarling."

HALF A SLIP IS BETTER THAN NONE

From Arizona: "You can have a drawer full of BEAUTI-FUL HALF SLIPS simply by cutting your lace-trimmed slips after they wear away around the tops and straps.

"There is a special nylon elastic which looks exactly like the elastic in underpants. You can sew it on around the waist, before cutting, and have a very pretty, neat job that will last indefinitely. Or, make a tubing and run elastic through the tube. It's neat.

"The elastic can be purchased at notion counters, and

comes with enough on a card for waist-banding two or three half slips."

PLASTIC SPOOL BAGS

From New Hampshire: "I found I was wasting too much time searching for just the right shade of thread when I kept SCADS OF SPOOLS in one drawer in no kind of order. I finally solved my problem by making good use of plastic sandwich bags!

"I sorted the thread by color, putting all the blues in one bag, the reds and various shades of pink in another, and so forth.

"Now it is a simple and timesaving act to reach for the bag containing the right color.

"This same idea works for seam bindings, bias tapes, and rickrack."

PASTRY BRUSH SWEEPS CLEAN

From Kentucky: "Since I make the majority of my own and my daughter's clothes you can bet my sewing machine is busy, and would always be full of LINT if I did not keep a small nylon pastry brush in my machine drawer. Whenever the lint collects, I simply sweep it off. Works marvelously!"

CUT 'N' SEW

From Florida: "Get a big square of nylon net, fold it catty-corner, and use it for a head scarf! This is fabulous in the summer, as the net is not hot.

"This NET SCARF may be folded up and put in your purse, and it never seems to wrinkle like the silk or cotton ones.

"My daughter cut some squares of net, decorated them

with cotton fringe bought at the dime store, and with the sewing machine made head squares for all of her girl friends for birthday presents.

"These scarves make wonderful items to pile up in your surprise closet for showers and other occasions. They can be made in any color.

"The cost, about 15 cents per scarf."

"When I make a new dress for my four-year-old, I use the scraps to make her a MATCHING PURSE.

"I use a round plastic detergent container for the base. I cut the top off the container, leaving the bottom about four inches tall.

"Next, I cut a piece of material the shape of the bottom, plus a seam's width. Then I cut a straight piece, long enough to go around the bottom piece of material and as wide as the plastic is tall, allowing an additional five inches for a hem at the top. I sew the pieces together, hem and stitch a seam to make a casting for a drawstring. Insert cord or tape for drawstring."

From Hawaii: "I buy remnants of slipcover material for about 50 cents a yard and make the sharpest SLIPCOVER BERMUDAS you have ever seen for 50 cents, plus the zipper!

"Instead of cutting the material lengthwise, I cut the width and get both pieces of the pattern from one width.

"No one believes my Bermudas cost so little because they look so expensive and wear so beautifully.

"One can also make slacks this way."

SOME SMOOTH NOTIONS

From Kentucky: "Take old nylon stockings and LINE THE SLEEVES in wool sweaters. Just cut the stocking the proper length and hand-sew one end to the cuff and the other end to the armhole.

"This is a wonderful idea for those who do not like the feel of scratchy sweaters on their bare arms. Besides the sweater is much easier to put on."

"I keep ready-made spray starch handy to use when pressing new materials and *before* cutting!

"It gives body, especially to very soft fabric, and helps PREVENT RAVELING and stretching too."

What do you do for a ZIPPER that just will not go up and down?

If the garment is dark, try taking a lead pencil and rub up and down on the zipper. Then zip it three or four times. The graphite will make it slide more easily.

If the clothing is white, I suggest you take a dab of old white wax candle and try that.

Both work. I've tried 'em.

MEMOS FROM THE MISCELLANEOUS FILE

To PRESERVE METAL FINISH on such things as earrings, bracelets, handbag clasps, belt buckles, etc., before using them, apply one or two coats of clear nail polish.

If this is repeated every six months, they will look like new for ages.

To KEEP PANTS FROM WEARING OUT AT THE CUFF, attach a piece of iron-on tape to the inside of the back of the cuff so the shoe will strike the tape instead of the pants cuff.

"I save the shirt cardboards and plastic bags from the laundry. When we take a trip I use them to keep BLOUSES NEAT. Just fold the blouses on the cardboards in the same manner in which shirts are folded, put them in the plastic bags, and they will stay fresh and unwrinkled. Saves on ironing."

From Georgia: "After I use up a large-size-thread spool of thread, I straighten the hook of a wire clothes hanger, thread the empty spool over the wire and bend the hook into place again. The spool KEEPS COLLARS UNWRINKLED when placed on the hanger."

Washing Well

DON'T BE A WASTEFUL WASHER

There will always be women who think that clean clothes result from putting heaps of detergent and ounce upon gurgling ounce of bleach into their washing machines. This simply is not so. Too much soap turns things gray, too much bleach is highly destructive.

Just think of all you waste by using *too much*. That expensive detergent plus your clothes and linens too.

Now, once again, ladies, here's how to do it right. Fill your washer with clothes to the recommended (usually three-quarters-full) capacity. All loads, of course, are sorted; white loads strictly white.

As for your detergent (or soap), I think it's a good idea to try different brands until you're satisfied, and even to try new brands as they appear. With whatever brand you are using, follow directions on the box. If you think you may be in the habit of using too much detergent, force yourself to put in half the usual amount. And the same for bleach, which should be added only after the washer is filled with water. Use just enough bleach and detergent so that your fingers feel slippery in the water. Put clothes through the wash cycle, then rinse. The white load (nonshrinkables, that is) should be rinsed in very hot water, not cold. If clothes have built up a gray film from too much detergent, add vinegar to the rinse water for several successive washings and the gray will disappear.

Well, there you are. Just a common sense method, but many women have found that these simple steps remarkably prolong the life of their washables.

Folks, always treat spots *before* you throw your clothes into the washer. Otherwise the hot water may set them for good. I had a gem of a letter from a lady in South Carolina who solved one spot problem beautifully:

"I had two small BLOOD SPOTS on the knee part of my denim pedal pushers.

"In order to get the blood spots out, I rubbed an ice cube on them. As I did this, I held a washcloth underneath. It worked perfectly!

"It took only about five minutes. The blood stains went on into the washcloth. Amazing.

"People who have fresh blood spots on clothing might try this method. I found it completely satisfactory."

Ladies, you may not believe it, but I actually pricked my finger to get some blood spots on a piece of cotton cloth. I let it dry for three hours. I then folded up a washcloth and put it under the spots. I picked up an ice cube and rubbed briskly over the spots, up and down, crosswise, and around and around, and do you know what? That blood left the cotton cloth and came out on that old washcloth!

And I also wonder if you all know that unseasoned meat tenderizer when mixed with a little water into a paste will remove old blood stains? Rub in, let set 30 minutes and wash as usual. If the spot has been there a long time, it may take more than one application.

And hey there, all you spaghetti eaters . . .

For those who get SPAGHETTI SPOTS on white garments: Recently, I had on a favorite drip-dry dress, and I was eating spaghetti.

You guessed it, the spaghetti hit my dress! I immediately picked up a piece of lemon, dampened my napkin in some water, and punched it into a piece of lemon. This allowed the lemon to absorb into the fibers of the cotton napkin. I took this lemon-dipped fabric and rubbed the spaghetti stain. It vanished before I could say "out, out, stubborn spaghetti spot."

So, I suggest that any of you who get a spaghetti stain on any white cotton or "lon" clothing, immediately find a piece of lemon (and I'll bet that vinegar will do the same thing) and wipe the spot off the garment. Then rinse in clear water.

WHY YOU SHOULDN'T OVERLOAD

You accomplish nothing by overloading your washing machine. The clothes come out almost as soiled as when they went in, and that's not the worst of it. In top-loading machines, the agitator that is working so hard to move the mass of wash only creates wear at the points where it rubs against the articles, sometimes even breaking the fibers.

So don't be tempted to make one load do the work of two. Depending on the type of machine you have (top or side loading) the clothes should begin swishing around freely as soon as the agitator or cylinder starts to move. If it does not, you have overloaded your machine and should take some articles out.

BYE, LINE

If you scrub and scrub the soil line on shirt collars, you will only shorten the life of the shirt. Along the line where the collar meets the neck or the cuff meets the wrist the fabric picks up a mixture of the usual soiling elements, plus body oil. It's the oil that makes the line hard to get out. Here's how to treat it. Rub first with a mild solvent— spot remover is fine. Then put the garment into the wash as usual. You can give that line a little extra soaping if you like, but the line should disappear without scrubbing.

Another solution to the problem is ordinary white blackboard chalk. This absorbs the grease and whitens the fabric besides. Just rub plenty of it in and set the article aside, overnight if possible. Next day, launder as usual.

SOS

"I am so ashamed of my baby daughter's stained undershirts, that I am tempted to discard them and buy new ones (which I can't afford to do) unless you can tell me how to remove those horrible stains. Please answer my distress signal."

I poured one gallon of hot water in a plastic wastebasket (enamel or stainless steel containers are acceptable but NOT aluminum) and added one-half cup of electric dishwasher compound (this is the stuff used in electric dishwashers) and one-fourth cup of bleach and stirred it well.

I then put my *100%* WHITE COTTON garments in this, let them soak for 30 minutes, then washed as usual. I used some vinegar in the rinse water. The garments came out snow white.

I have taken stained pillowslips—that were really yellow and badly soiled and, after using this method, they were as white as snow!

If you use this on WHITE uniforms which contain nylon, etc., do NOT put them in HOT water as it sets wrinkles.

Pour hot water over the dishwashing compound granules and let it get cool BEFORE you put your "lons" in.

Do NOT stir the mixture while the clothes are soaking.

I sent a copy of this method to one of the top chemists in Washington, and here is his answer:

"We have found this a very effective method of whitening badly stained garments.

"We tested various dishwashing compounds according to your procedure. In every case the fabric was either lightened or completely whitened. In each case, we worked ONLY on stained WHITE fabrics, as obviously the chlorine bleach may react with some colored dyes.

"Upon removal from the bleach solution, vinegar will help neutralize any compound agent left in the fabric."

Now, I think this is about one of the greatest discoveries in a long time. It is especially great on dingy pillow slips. We tested many and the results were amazing though they had been laundered commercially for months.

I think it would be an excellent idea to use the above method for T-shirts too! We tried it on babies' undershirts and it was great. And what about those white cotton socks with their stubborn dirt?

Do NOT keep reusing the same mixture once it has become discolored. Pour this out and make fresh mixture again. And isn't it exciting to have really white laundry?

STARCHING CLOTHES

A launderess wrote in an idea for those who make a big batch of cooked starch each week, and must strain it because it's lumpy, gotten too cold, etc.

If they will take an old nylon stocking, lay it in a bowl, pour the warm starch through the leg opening and let it drain into the bowl, it will give perfectly strained starch.

By holding the stocking up after the starch cools, you can run your hand down the stocking, from top to bottom, and squeeze out every iota.

It seems to me that tea strainers and flour sifters do not remove all of the tiny lumps, and those minute pieces in the starch are what cause spots on dark clothes.

When starching lots of pieces, it's far cheaper to make your own starch.

I'm told by authorities that spray starches are about seven times as expensive as liquid and liquid ones are about seven times as expensive as dry and pre-cooked flakes. But their convenience does follow the order of their cost.

If you have lots of starching to do make up a big batch, pour it in your washing machine and use your spin dryer. Pour some in an old spray bottle and spray as you iron for heavier spot starching.

But if you're real smart as soon as you hang your clothes on the line you will get your spray bottle and give it those extra squirts then and there. Saves time in the long run.

When you make hot starch, you have to let it cool before you can stick your hands in it. Then scum usually forms on top. To prevent this . . . put some ice cubes on top of the goop. As the ice melts, it will form a thin film of water and keep the thick scum from forming.

And last but not least:

Always use spray starch on the wrong side of dark clothes. Helps prevent spots. If you do get a starch streak on something, put an ice cube in a washrag and rub it off and keep ironing. Saves time.

PLUMBER'S FRIEND

"What in the world is a plumber's friend, and why should I buy one?

A plumber's friend (I am guessing where it got its name) is really everybody's friend, and ordinarily what is used to unclog drains. It has a wooden handle attached to a rubber suction cup.

I suggest that housewives buy one (they cost very little) at the supermarket, hardware or dime store.

The short-handled ones are best for us because, besides being cheaper, they have many household uses other than those for which they were intended.

We all have a few things to wash out, and don't like to "fire" up the washing machine for just a few items.

Here's where our plumber's friend comes in:

Just put the items in the sink, wash basin, or wastebasket, add water and detergent, and squish them up and down with the plunger. Rinse them the same way.

Socks should be washed in water heated to at least 140 degrees, and wives (or bachelors, for that matter) don't want to stick their hands in water that hot.

So . . . let the plunger do the work.

Fantabulous!

I also recommend, after buying one of these little gadgets, that you take a paring knife and make three or four V-shaped cuts on the top of it. This will let the soiled water (which you are plunging) escape as you push down on it. Then, clean water will come into the clothing as you pull up on it.

In addition to washing the socks, this gadget is excellent for washing curtains, underwear and baby clothes that cannot be put into the washing machine, or anything else that must be hand-washed.

Never put your hands into hot water and detergent suds if you can avoid it. We can't buy those "hands-men-love-to-touch" at any price—but everybody can afford one of those little "friends."

Why not run (don't walk) to your nearest store and buy one? You'll find it to be one of the most valuable friends you have.

I sure do.

DRYCLEANING

"Our drycleaning business is over 100 years old. With reference to cleaning curtains and draperies, here is why we have to accept them at 'owner's risk':

"Many fabrics have white or very light backgrounds, which become yellow and streaky from sun, household smoking, furnace gases, and general exposure.

"If an afternoon's exposure on a sunny day at the beach

can burn us, then what must happen to curtains and draperies hanging at windows for weeks and months?

"Curtains at windows which are never open can develop water marks—*cold* fabric condenses water the same as glass panes.

"Novelty fabrics, of course, are created solely for appearance and not for durability. Many "wash and wear" fabrics stand up well if dipped in the tub every other week or two, but do not react as well when left hanging a year before being sent to the cleaner.

"The actual damage is done at the window and does not become apparent until the cleansing and finishing.

"Many of today's curtain and drapery fabrics do shrink, in spite of our best efforts to keep them to size, even with special stretching equipment. Why not be prepared for such shrinkage, and have extra wide hems, so that you or your decorator could let out the extra material when being cleaned?

"Examine your curtains and draperies carefully at least every other month. Dust them or vacuum them periodically. You may be surprised at their condition!"

FIBERGLASS IS FRAGILE

DON'T put anything made of FIBERGLASS in your washing machine with any other article of clothing.

This fabric is just what it says—glass!

You cannot put an article of clothing in with this material and then expect to wear it again.

Fiberglass breaks the same as a glass dropped on the floor, and those little glass fibers get into your wash mixture and into any other clothing in the machine. These small glass fibers can cause serious irritation.

If this has already happened to you, and you have to see your doctor, be sure to tell him you washed your clothing in a washer along with something made of fiberglass.

BE GENTLE WITH BELTS

From Rhode Island: "BELTS belonging to cotton dresses should be whisked through suds, not water. Rinse buckle first, then dry immediately by pulling through a piece of toweling or a folded paper towel.

"Then hang the belt on a nail or hook so that the full length hangs straight.

"Helps prevent cracks in belt backing."

WASH SWEATERS

"This is the best way I have found to wash and shape those big, thick, loosely woven sweaters that are so fashionable nowadays:

"I used to wash as usual according to the instructions, but they always stretched from the weight of the water. So I have learned to squeeze them gently and then roll them in a heavy bath towel to take out any excess water.

"I then toss the sweater in the air and catch it 20 or 30 times.

"This fluffs the yarn and puts the stitches back in place.

"You may then shape the sweater on a towel to dry. Your sweater will look brand new. It's absolutely beautiful."

Now folks, don't you dare laugh at our dear friend. She's found a good answer to those loose-knit sweaters.

My daughter has one. I have washed it often and finally

tried this method. Sure enough, by tossing it lightly and catching it, it does get air into those tiny, loosely woven wool fibers. I even found that the sweater dried quicker, too.

Another thing I found good about this hint was that I got the most exercise I had had in a month of Sundays! It's practically like playing "jacks" again.

So try it next time you wash your sweater. I'm sure you'll love it as much as I do. It works on any kind of knitted sweater. Fantastic!

SWEATER KNOTS

The Agriculture Department says, "Pills belong in bottles . . . not on sweaters!"

You can reduce pilling by turning the garment inside out when you wash it, and for further protection . . . place it in a mesh bag before laundering it.

If it already has pills . . . you can remove them one by one. . . .

But . . .

First, use fine sandpaper and gently sand those knots.

If they are stubborn and aren't removed by sanding, pull the cloth firmly over a curved surface (so the pills stand up away from the material) then cut them off carefully with your scissors or a safety razor.

WHITE COTTON GLOVES

"I am a secretary.

"To look well groomed, it is necessary that I wear a fresh pair of white cotton gloves every day.

"After trying every method I know, including three kinds of bleaches, the laundry, and the drycleaner's, with no success . . . please help."

You're not alone!

After working with a chemist recently, we have dis-covered the answer to what we call "whiter than white":

Put two quarts of the hottest water that will come out of your faucet into a glass or plastic container. Add one-fourth cup of dishwashing compound (the type used in electric dishwashers), then add about two tablespoons of household bleach, and stir.

Put your white cotton gloves in and let soak for 30 minutes. Do not keep on using this mixture once it has become discolored. Make a new batch.

And, hon, since you are "Little Miss Snow White," rinse the gloves in a mixture of one quart of water and one-fourth cup of vinegar.

Now, here's the secret:

Do not wring out the gloves. Just smooth them, palm side up, on porcelain, such as the edge of the bathtub. This will do the most professional ironing job you have ever seen.

WHITE WAYS FOR TENNIS SHOES

We all know that TENNIS SHOES are made to be worn, but letting them get *too* dirty makes them wear out sooner. The best way to care for them is to keep them clean with weekly washings.

Here is the easiest way I have found to wash white tennis shoes: Remove the strings and tie them, in a loose knot, through an eyelet in the shoe. Put the shoes in your washing machine along with your bath towels. Let them run through the whole cycle.

The buffing they get from the towels really cleans them up.

Hang them on the clothesline by clipping a clothespin to

the tongue of the shoe. This will allow the moisture to run to the back of the heel.

(If you want to polish them, do so as soon as they are taken from the washing machine, diluting your polish with at least four parts of water. Then hang to dry.)

After they are dry, spray them with a little spray starch. They will stay cleaner longer. Besides, the soil will wash off easier the next time.

From Florida: "I find it timesaving and very helpful to polish WHITE CANVAS SHOES as soon as I take them from the washer and while they are still soaking wet. Not only does this prevent streaking, but when they are dry, they are ready to wear with no second handling necessary."

SOME SUDS!

From Nevada: "If you take a hot ice pick and make a hole in the handle of either a half-gallon or a one-gallon plastic BLEACH bottle (about one inch from the pouring spout), the bleach will pour out smoothly, and no more spattering."

This is the discovery of the century!

I flitted to the kitchen in jig-time to try this one. It works. Fantabulously. . . . Instead of that ol' bleach going "blub-blub" in spurts, it poured out like the fountain of youth.

Be sure to make the hole on *top* of the handle about one inch from the neck of the plastic bleach bottle.

"I am in college and must do my own LAUNDRY. Rather than carry a box of detergent and a box of dry bleach down to the automatic laundry, I measure out what I need and put the mixture in a white cotton sock, using one sock for each load.

"A safety pin or loose knot tied at the top of the sock will keep the detergent from spilling until time to use it. Just pour the contents of one sock into the machine and let 'er roll."

From Ohio: "Please tell me how to get rid of SUDS when the washing machine is overloaded and the suds are pouring out all over the floor. I've never seen such a mess!"

Sprinkle salt out of a box onto the suds and into the water. Just watch these suds disappear.

EASIER DRYING

From Connecticut: "If a person has a wringer-type washer as I do and no spin dryer, speed up the DRYING PROCESS by adding to the dryer one or two dry, heavy, clean bath towels. This helps absorb the moisture and I find that my clothes dry in far less time."

From Michigan: "During the summer months when I hang the wash outdoors, I find the following procedure to be quite a time-saver: I turn all my SOCKS right side out and hang them around the top of my plastic basket and

111

through the spokes so that they do not blow away. When clothes are harvested from the line, socks are all ready for taking indoors.

"They dry beautifully."

This one's a lulu! Prevents marks on socks from clothespins, saves energy pinning each one on the line and removing it, adds clothesline space, etc. Just for fun, stop a minute right now and figure out how many socks you wash each week and multiply that by fifty-two, then by the number of years you expect to live! Amazing! Think of the time you could save by using this method.

From Vermont: "When laundering GIRDLES which I hang on the line, I button the garters over the line, eliminating the sharp crease on the edge of the girdle caused by clothespins."

"Here's a wonderful way to hasten the drying of LINGERIE: Tie one end of a large plastic dry-cleaner bag and pull the open end over lingerie and hanger.

"Slip your hair-dryer hose in the open end of the plastic bag and press the bag around the hose nozzle.

"Use florists' wire or pipe cleaners to hold the bag

securely around the hose, turn on the dryer, and your lingerie will be dry in a jiffy.

"Be sure to leave a small hole in the top of the bag, or tie it loosely, so excess air can escape."

From Pennsylvania: "Never throw away your old shower-curtain rings or pins.

"Keep some of the curtain rings on your CLOTHESLINE at all times. Then if you want to dry something on a hanger, place the hanger hook through the shower pin and bend the hook a little, and the hanger will never blow off the line.

"To hang up venetian blinds to dry, hook the pins over the rod in the blind fixture, one on each end. Wonderful.

"Pants stretchers hook into them nicely, too.

"Last but not least, after you wash your lampshades, hang them on the shower pins.

"I could not do without them."

THE TRICK IS IN THE HANGING

"I have found a way to keep the front of my wash-and-wear dresses from clinging to the back (or is it vice versa?) while they are drying.

"I put a PLASTIC BAG on the hanger, then put the wet dress over it.

"The bag helps the dress dry faster and more wrinkle-free (since it isn't clinging together), and there is no danger of rust stains from the hanger."

"Here is a little hint for those who have to hang clothes outside on the line in very cold weather:

"I put on a pair of woolen GLOVES, then put my rubber

gloves over these, making sure that my fingers are pushed far down into the tips of the gloves.

"This not only keeps my hands dry, but also warm. It sounds clumsy, but is not nearly as clumsy as wet, cold fingers."

"As manufacturers of TROUSER CREASERS for over a quarter of a century, we think our suggestion is the quickest and easiest way to use them:

"This calls for hanging the wet trousers on the clothesline by the waistband.

"After the trousers are securely pinned to the line, hang the required number of creaser frames over your shoulder and go down the line inserting one frame into each trouser leg.

"After the frames are all in place, go back along the line and tighten and adjust them to the proper crease.

"Blue jeans should have the creasers inserted *sideways* since the material usually doesn't hold a crease anyway, but this way at least the wrinkles can be stretched away."

From Arkansas: "With a houseful of sheer CURTAIN PANELS, I find it far easier to wash them and put them directly back on the windows while they are still wet.

"I only do half of the panels in each room at one time.

"I spread one damp panel (open full width) on the curtain rod and insert the curtain rod from another window in the bottom hem. After they dry they are beautiful. No ironing required.

"If you want the curtains starched you can use spray starch. Just lift the bottom curtain rod, hold the curtain at a forty-five degree angle, and spray away.

"By pulling the bottom of the curtain out from the window, the starch will hit it at an angle and not get on your windows.

"Be sure to place several thicknesses of newspaper on the floor under the curtains to catch any water that might drip."

From Idaho: "I keep my woolen BLANKETS from shrinking after washing by putting them on my curtain stretchers to dry. The blankets come out in their original shape. Gently brush the pinholes which are left along the sides, and the holes will disappear immediately."

SPRINKLER SYSTEM

From Georgia: "I have found the most wonderful way to sprinkle my clothes with no work at all!

"I just hang my laundry on the clothesline overnight and LET THE DEW DO THE DAMPENING! In the morning, the clothes are just right to iron.

"There are fewer wrinkles and, best of all, no baskets of clothes sitting around waiting for me to sprinkle them.

"If it happens to rain, then just wait until they are partly dry. The most important thing is that they are dampened evenly."

From Oklahoma: "You may think I'm crazy, but I DAMPEN CLOTHES IN THE SHOWER.

"I turn the shower on hot and just whip the clothes under it, one article at a time until they're just damp enough to iron, then roll and let set awhile.

"I don't have enough space to spread clothes out to be sprinkled, but this method is so quick and handy, I don't think I'd use the space if I had it."

You're not crazy. You just found a quicker way! And look at the exercise you're getting!

From California: "The CLOTHES SPRINKLER I like best is one I made by taking a five-cent sprinkler top (with cork around the base) and putting it in the opening of a plastic liquid detergent bottle.

"It is squeezable, and holds enough water to dampen my basket of clothes without refilling."

IRON-EASYS

"For those who want to IRON CURTAINS after a wash job, and usually get them too wet, not wet enough, or wet in spots while they are still dry in others—here's an idea:

"I put my curtains back in my dryer (even though they have been in the ironing basket for a week or so), wet a bath towel and partially wring it out. Then I turn on the dryer at the proper heat, and let them tumble for about five minutes along with the dampened towel.

"This seems to create a steam which soaks into the fibers of the curtains, and makes for perfect ironing every time."

From Utah: "When you are IRONING and need a sleeve board, just roll a terry cloth towel around your rolling pin!

"A sleeve will go over that little old rolling pin like a glove, and the rolling pin turns as you iron each side of the sleeve, thus preventing a crease."

"My husband wears work shirts with heavy advertising embroidered on the back. I find it far easier to IRON the lettering from the wrong side first, then just press the right side.

"I ironed these shirts for years before I figured out the easier way."

WONDERFUL STARCH

It's such a pleasure to put on an article of clothing that is not simply clean and fresh, but expertly starched as well. Neatness lasts longer, and when you're finally ready to return it to the wash, it comes clean faster.

Starching isn't half the trouble some people think, especially if you do it this speedy way . . . in the washing machine!

Prepare your starch in the strength you want. For normal starching of entire garments, a thin mixture is best, and be sure there are no lumps. After the clothes to be starched have gone through the spin cycle, pour into the machine enough water and starch in the recommended proportions to saturate all the items. Set the dial so that the machine will run dry for about three minutes. The motion will distribute the starch quite evenly throughout all the articles.

Now, if you want certain parts of these garments to have a heavier application of starch, have it ready as you take them from the machine. Then just spot-starch the collars, cuffs, etc., with the heavier mixture, or with permanent starch, as you prefer.

From Hawaii: "When I iron, I spray extra STARCH on the seat of my children's playsuits, shorts, and jeans. If they slide in the mud, I can just throw the clothes in the washer and they come out like new. The starch keeps the soil from grinding into the fabric and it washes out like a breeze."

From South Carolina: "Instead of STARCHING my doilies, I spray them with clear plastic spray starch, shape them, and allow to dry thoroughly.

"They hold their shape even when I wash them."

From Georgia: "I wonder if any of your readers have ever STARCHED their pot holders. You'd be surprised how much longer they stay clean, and the grease doesn't soak in, either. Just a little spray starch works fine!"

Folks, this sure works. The pot holders do last longer between washes. Besides, you should see how easily the soil washes out when using this method!

"For the homemaker who likes spray STARCH, may I suggest liquid starch diluted to desired strength in an old spray bottle. I've found it easier on the budget and you are less likely to run out of starch in the middle of the ironing.

"I use two separate bottles. I fill one with a *stronger* starch for collars and cuffs, and the other with *regular* starch for the rest of my ironing. I label the bottles with adhesive tape."

WASH-IN COMFORT

"Fabric softeners, when added to the final rinse of the washing cycle of your machine, will help ELIMINATE STATIC ELECTRICITY in clothing."

From West Virginia: "After repeated washings, babies' plastic pants become stiff and uncomfortable. To KEEP THE PANTS SOFT, take them from the washer and pop them into the dryer with a full load of towels. This will even soften stiff plastic pants."

LAUNDER-AIDS

From Louisiana: "We know that inexpensive woven clothes baskets often come apart in a short time. How about investing a little more for one that will last a lot longer?

"Buy a large, heavy wicker basket and spray it with a can of enamel. Your ENAMEL BASKET can be washed with hot suds and there will be no more black marks on clothes from a mildewed woven basket that absorbs moisture."

From Connecticut: "I converted an old shower curtain into a couple of laundry bags.

"I used the upper half of the curtain, cutting the bottom half off. I then cut the top half in two pieces, folded each piece in half, and sewed across the bottom and sides.

"I inserted a cord drawstring through the holes where the shower hooks are attached. I use the drawstring to close the bags.

"These SHOWER-CURTAIN LAUNDRY BAGS can also hold your dampened laundry."

INSTEAD OF DOING A SLOW BURN

From Pennsylvania: "When my son attended college, he brought his LAUNDRY home every weekend.

"I would iron it very nicely and hang it on the clothes rod in his car, but by the time he arrived back at school, his clothes had slid from one end of the rod to the other and were a sorry mess.

"To solve this problem, I went to the dime store and bought an inexpensive dog chain. I used wire hangers and hung my son's clothes in the small loops of the chain and thus avoided a constant sliding of his clothes. Also, the clothes could be spaced so as not to obstruct his driving view."

From Alabama: "To relieve your mind of worry about having left the electric iron on, use a double socket where you plug the iron in. Plug in a small RED LIGHT in the other socket.

"I worked in a store where the fire insurance company demanded the use of such a red light. It works for me in my home."

REALLY RE-MARK-ABLE

From Pennsylvania: "We use colored felt pens to mark the tops of new NYLON HOSE.

"As one stocking becomes unwearable, it is easy to find its mate by looking at the pen mark on top. (There are so many similar colors, it is often difficult to distinguish them after many washings.)

"If you have many pairs of stockings, and not enough different colors of felt pens to go around, use different designs, numbers or letters.

"In our house there are six girls wearing nylons now, and we use both their initials and a color mark to identify the hosiery.

"No problems or arguments; if one of our girls has on another's stockings (can and does happen!), the mark is a dead giveaway!"

From South Carolina: "Here's how I keep SOCKS straight for my three small boys:

"The youngest boy wears striped socks, the middle one a diamond pattern, and the oldest has argyles.

"This system is so simple that my daughters now enjoy helping me sort their brothers' socks."

DO RIGHT BY NYLON

I know a young bride who turned all her lovely new lingerie pink in the very first wash she did. She threw it in with the bath towels you see, and it seems her mother had never mentioned to her the folly of such a short cut.

Now, everybody listen! Nylon is a synthetic fabric that readily absorbs dye. This has advantages: You needn't worry about a nylon garment running in the wash. But it will, especially if it is white, take on a hue from any other article that releases color into the wash water. So wash nylon by itself. Anything that lasts as long as nylon should be cared for lovingly, right?

Nylon, Dacron, and fiberglass curtains will come out of the wash with more body if you put in a half-cup of powdered milk into the rinse water. Well, why not?

121

Don't waste time untangling shirts after taking them from the wash. Before you throw them into the machine, just button the cuffs to a couple of buttons on the front. Cross my heart, it works!

TYING KNOTS IN NYLON STOCKINGS

"That idea of tying nylon stockings in loose knots when removing them is terrific!

"I knot my stockings gently and loosely above the ankle when I take them off and the foot part is free to be washed thoroughly.

"I have since learned to put this loose knot gently over the middle of a plastic coat hanger and when they are dry, I hang the coat hanger and all in my closet. I can see at a glance which stockings I want."

What we said was: "A wonderful way to keep our nylon stockings sorted and in perfect order is to knot pairs gently around the knee of the stockings when taking them off. Leave the knot in while you wash the stockings. They dry beautifully this way, and no more searching later for the mates."

Another thing, if you have stockings with runners in them, tie them near the ankle and you will know that those are pairs which are not in perfect condition.

And did you know that if you fasten the BACK supporter on your girdle first, then the front one, that your stocking seams will stay straight?

And for those with heavy thighs . . . sew an extra supporter on each side of your girdle. This will give you extra support and your stockings aren't likely to slide off, pop or slip when you stoop, bend and sit!

122

Spotlessly Yours

One of the best favors a housewife can do herself is to learn to clean with as little expenditure of energy as necessary. The jobs get done just the same, and you have energy left for husband, kids, friends. The following hints can save you hours upon hours over the years, plus the dollars that mount up from using the inexpensive but efficient cleaning materials that are suggested.

SPRING HOUSECLEANING?

I've always been swamped with letters about spring cleaning. I want to help all of you, but I better make it clear right here that I don't believe in spring cleaning! The best I can do is tell you what I know and practice. It will not apply to all of you.

I am not a fanatic, although I admit I used to be one. Some of us were born that way or our mothers were. Or a neighbor said to us, "Have you done your spring cleaning?" DON'T let this bother you!

If this ever happens look her straight in the eye and say, "My house is always clean." *Then smile!*

I don't figure it is anyone's business whether my house is clean or not. Do you? Why should you beat your brains out with waxes, polishes and scouring powders twice a year? This takes weeks if you let it all pile up. Then you *are* pooped.

I NEVER do spring housecleaning. (Or fall, for that matter.) I clean the year round. My home is neat, clean, in order, and I have a place for everything and everything is in its place.

I find that if any task or chore is done when one is in the mood . . . it not only gets the job done quicker, but better. Also, it is done with pleasure and love and not labeled: Drudgery.

Did you know that many women do housework at midnight? They do! When they can't sleep, they get up and do the laundry and iron and clean that linen closet or kitchen cabinet.

Some women think everything in the house should be washed two or three times a year. This includes washing all furniture to remove waxes, washing lampshades, taking beds apart, and cleaning all knickknacks. This is their privilege! When they die, they won't know how much their husbands spend on a cleaning woman! Or who his next wife might be!

But these women will have passed on leaving immaculate houses. Bless 'em. The trouble with most women is that they try to outdo each other! They try to have the cleanest house, the shiniest car, the prettiest hat, the biggest diamonds, the nicest living room, but most of all, try to out-brag each other.

It's like a slap in the face with a wet dish towel when another woman says, "Whew, I have just turned my house upside down and it's spotless. I just finished my spring cleaning."

But . . . dear friends, she usually says this to you over a bridge table, or at a dinner party when she is all dressed up and you wonder . . . how could she possibly?

Perhaps she did but . . .

Ask yourself this: WHY was her house so dirty that she had to turn it upside down?

Here's a bit of advice to young mothers with children: Don't let these women upset you. Nothing inflates a woman's ego so much as deflating another woman! The woman who makes these remarks usually has no children (or the children are married) and she has nothing else to think about.

Keep in mind that no woman can tie two shoes at the same time. If you doubt this . . . try it! She looks just like you without her girdle and make-up! Her beds are unmade in the morning. She still has dishes to wash and laundry to do. And she looks awful, too, with her hair in rollers!

All you can do is your best. You can't even do that if you are worked to death and try to keep up with the Joneses. Live and forget about the Joneses. They don't pay your bills and sit up at night with your sick baby. Be yourself. Let loose. Just try to please your own immediate family. There will never be *anyone* in your home any better.

Quit comparing yourself with others. No need to! Each of us is different. Don't try to go by standards! Who dictated those standards? Your *mother*, or your *neighbor?* You are NOT your mother and you are certainly not your neighbor.

Sure . . . I could tell you to make the beds at 8:30, wash your dishes at 9:00, do your laundry on Mondays, iron on Tuesdays, wax floors the first of each month, wash windows every three months, clean venetian blinds at least three times a year or the tapes will rot . . . not so!

Keep this in mind. When mother was a bride she didn't paint her kitchen, pay the bills, wash the car, mow the lawn, build the sandpile for junior and paper the house.

If your house is kept top-cleaned, then this allows for *deep* cleaning when you are IN THE MOOD whether it's spring or not. Take advantage of the strength you have when you are angry or annoyed at the world in general (and who doesn't have those days?)

Use THIS energy to clean closets, wash blinds, wax furniture, sort clothes, get rid of clutter . . . especially that storage closet, garage, and the attic!

Sweep under your beds, vacuum the drapes (I don't care if it's midnight), clean those shelves and your sewing basket . . . when you are in the *mood* or *mad*. Then you won't have that *heavy* spring cleaning.

Just because it is spring and your neighbor is doing her semiannual cleaning doesn't mean that it's time to clean YOUR house. Maybe your neighbor has had troubles and has decided NOW is the time. YOUR spring might come in the fall. Or midwinter! Who cares? I don't.

I know lots of women have rigid rules for spring cleaning. Slipcovers, for instance, are a very sore subject.

Some people write that they remove all their rugs and put on their slipcovers a certain time of the year.

So . . . it is a must for THEM. But just because people put on their slipcovers in the spring, doesn't mean *you* have to! Have you ever thought to put on your summer slipcovers in the winter? I do! I find that it is a relief to put my slipcovers on every two months or so . . . winter or summer!

Rugs are another sore subject. Those of you who have *"heard"* that you have to have summer and winter rugs . . . ask yourself Why??? If your living room is used more in the summer and you feel that it is a *waste* to use your best rug in the living room . . . switch rugs and put that living room rug in your bedroom for the summer (or any season for that matter) and get relief. And change. I have. I like changes—it relieves boredom.

Sometimes, I want to work in the garden . . . so I work for a day and plant seeds. Other days I am in the sewing mood . . . then I patch all the linen, and sew. Other days I am in the mood to cook . . . then I really fill up my freezer.

But always remember, dear darlings, most things that are done best are done when one is in the mood! If spring housecleaning hits you on your birthday and your birthday is in February . . . do it then! Do what YOU want to. Please your family. This is a wife's *first* duty.

I am not going to tell you to sweep under your bed *every* day. I don't. I am lucky if I hit that spot once a week. But then I don't live where there is a lot of dust; I have carpets; the street is paved (which solves lots of dust problems), and I don't let my work stack up. If you live where there is a lot of dust . . . and have a phobia about dust under your beds . . . sweep under them six times a day, if it makes you feel better. There is no real answer! Each of us is different and lives under different conditions.

As for taking down beds and cleaning slats and springs . . . again comes the same answer. People who need this outlet . . . let them have their spring cleaning. Let them tear the house apart . . . we don't care. It's not our problem. We have our own. Yep, we all do!

I do not believe in doing laundry on Monday, ironing on Tuesday, baking on Wednesday, etc. Who knows if you are going to feel like doing laundry on Monday . . . it just might be raining or—you just might not feel like it. So let the laundry stay in the hamper. Who cares as long as you have clean clothes? Do it on Tuesday. That just might be the day you *are* in the mood!

When these moods hit, you should clean house. Get those closets clean, get rid of old clothes, mend, wax floors and wash venetian blinds.

But whatever you decide about cleaning . . . do it your way . . . Remember, YOU are YOU and others are others. Be yourself!

Do what you can when you can. But most of all, don't work yourself to death. Remember that if you die tomorrow, it is likely another woman will take over your household (whether it be a new wife, a mother, sister or mother-in-law) and she will use your best linen and china and wonder why you saved it.

Use what you HAVE today. Live today. Keep your family happy.

Ladies, the point of all this is to put you at ease and make you happy in your own home. And as for that old

spring cleaning—don't ever forget—all the furniture polish in the world won't put a gleam in your husband's eye!

BRING BACK THE CARPET SWEEPER

From Pennsylvania: "What's so old-fashioned about a
CARPET SWEEPER?

"In the old days, that's all grandmother could afford,
besides a broom and a feather duster!

"Using a carpet sweeper on your carpets each day (when
you are too tired, or don't have time to get out the electric
vacuum cleaner) helps to keep the rugs in good condition,
and is much better than not cleaning at all.

"Once dirt and dust settles on top of a rug, isn't it much
better to remove it with one of those magic gadgets, than
to leave it there for the family to walk over and grind down
into the carpet fibers?"

It certainly is! I have often advocated, preached, and
even yelled that every housewife needs a carpet sweeper
and a feather duster for emergencies. They are always
good to hit the high spots quickly and with very little effort
on your part. There are days when it takes energy to do
just "nothing," eh?

ICKY STICKY KITCHEN GOO

Let's discuss a subject that nobody likes . . . CLEANING
ABOVE KITCHEN CABINETS. What a mess! No matter how
clean the housewife is, this little storage shelf collects
more grease, carbon, and goo than one could possibly
imagine.

The day you try to clean the top of your cabinets, don't
plan anything else. If you get it done, and do it the right
way while you're at it, the next time will be far easier,
quicker and smoother.

Here's how: The best way I know of to remove the goo is to add one-half cup of kerosene to a pail of hot water. Use paper napkins or paper towels and dip them into this wonderful mixture and wipe away.

There is a reason for using paper napkins or paper towels instead of rags: It is the tendency of the housewife to keep on using a rag after it has become soiled. I suggest using paper products for this nasty job because once the paper gets dirty you throw it away and pick up a clean piece. Paper products, including facial tissues, are mighty cheap and they do not have to be washed.

In place of kerosene, I have found that a solution of ammonia and water (read directions on bottle) is also excellent for removing carbon. However, ammonia does have an odor, especially when we are working up high near the ceiling. Also, if the ammonia mixture is made too strong, it will remove paint! Especially if you have wooden cabinets.

After your cabinet tops are clean and rinsed thoroughly take a roll of inexpensive waxed paper and cover the top of the shelves. This will save you trouble for months to come.

Better yet, if you put two pieces of waxed paper—one on top of the other—the next time you clean you can just rip off the top piece. This will save you hours!

Then, and only then, replace the items you keep up there, such as turkey platters (this is a great place for platters as they don't fit many places), the vaporizer, big pieces of china, the waffle iron, etc. But never, never place anything up there without covering it with a piece of plastic. Garment bags are excellent for this. Mainly because they adhere to each article, and we get them free. Then, when it comes time to use something, all you have to do is remove the covering and it's clean as a whistle. This also saves washing those articles.

If you use this method of cleaning, the next time that icky sticky day comes around you can do the job in one-fourth the time.

Why waste time and elbow grease?

MORE KITCHEN CHORES

For those of you who have STAINLESS STEEL sinks, drainboards, hoods over your stoves, etc.:

As soon as you have finished doing the dishes, squeeze the dishrag or sponge out thoroughly, then rub it over a bar of soap, and use it to wipe across the backsplash and other stainless surfaces.

All the spots will be gone in a jiffy, and it makes the stainless steel shine like a mirror.

You should see how it works on a stainless steel stove! Great! Just rewipe with a dry cloth (which is not necessary on sinks and drainboards).

No need to polish stainless steel after doing this.

From Pennsylvania: "My problem is RUST SPOTS IN THE WHITE KITCHEN SINK. I know the cause but not the cure! I have tried scouring powder, sal soda, bleaches, etc., but to no avail. Any help will be appreciated."

Use liquid rust remover. Just squirt on and wipe away. Wash and rinse well. That's all there is to it.

DEFROSTING TRICKS

From New York: "I live in an efficiency apartment. Everyone in the building has a problem DEFROSTING THE REFRIGERATOR. What a job this is!

"Our main trouble is emptying the tray beneath the freezer compartment when it fills up with water. What a mess this is to empty. It always spills."

Answer? Don't empty it! Just turn the refrigerator back on and let the water form into solid ice again. Next day, take the tray to the bathtub or shower and dump the solid brick of ice. Let this melt. That's all there is to it! Sure saves mopping up the kitchen floor.

Once in a while we all get brainstorms . . .

A woman wrote in over a year ago (and I have been testing it monthly ever since):

When you defrost your refrigerator, *dry* the freezer compartment inside with a towel. And put shortening (solidified, NOT oil) on a paper napkin, and wipe the metal parts inside the freezing compartment. And, by golly, the next time you defrost, the ice will fall off like magic.

And, believe me, it works!

I have never seen where this would harm any refrigerator or deep freezer, provided you DO NOT USE SALTED FAT.

Do NOT use bacon drippings, salted butter or oleo, etc., because these contain salt, which we now know can ruin aluminum. Use ONLY solidified, unsalted shortening which comes in cans.

Next time you get ready to defrost, when you unplug

132

the refrigerator, the coils next to the metal immediately quit working. By golly, blocks and chunks of frost and ice just fall off as if a magic wand had been waved. Just gently use your pancake turner to remove them.

It sure saves defrosting time.

And, friends, as an added precaution:

NEVER hack away with an ice pick or knife at ice that won't come loose in a refrigerator or freezer. If you should hit a pipe (which many people have), the fumes can be extremely dangerous—to say nothing of the expensive repairs your box will need!

Just smear on this shortening. It's the easiest way.

REFRIGERATOR ODORS

"What causes horrible odors in my refrigerator and deep freezer?"

I discussed this with an authority who was an engineer in the business and here is his advice verbatim:

"Milk, or something of that order, usually has frozen and run down into the bottom of your refrigerator or freezer, gone through the seal *into* the insulation on top of the compressor and has soured, and this gives you this rank odor which one cannot get rid of by washing with soda, etc. The odor will get worse as time goes on.

"Oftentimes, refrigerators are too cold and milk freezes and overflows. This runs into the bottom of the box and eventually into the little crease between the bottom of the box and the outer ridge trim. Anything which might happen to overflow sours. When milk is set in the door of the refrigerator, each time you slam the door you take a chance of some of that milk spilling out and getting down into these little cracks.

"As 'this' grows with the heat of the motor, it causes a

most obnoxious odor, which you will never get rid of, even if you put vanilla, etc., inside the refrigerator.

"The *only* solution to this problem is to call a repairman and have the box taken apart, the old, sour-smelling insulation removed and new insulation put in.

"Sometimes fresh meat is put into a refrigerator and the blood will ooze out of the wrappings and the blood juices will form an odor in the box. When this happens, wash the box with a solution of vanilla and water or baking soda and water. Then the box must be aired completely for at *least* 24 hours with the door *open*, so that the box itself will thoroughly dry out, and the *chemical* reaction can take place.

"Women who have upright freezers with these odors, should also check the insulation packing in the door for impurities which have dripped down on the packing.

"What causes the terrific odor is that when the bacteria (this is whatever has dripped) drips on the batting (which is the filling and insulation), then the heat from the motor hits it when the box runs. It tends to culture the bacteria and makes it grow and become rank. Here is probably the answer to where most people get their rancid odor in a refrigerator or deep freezer which they cannot get rid of."

And, folks, *please* if you've got a deep freezer *don't* go off on a vacation and turn off all the electricity. *Remember* your freezer is full of expensive food.

CLEAN KITCHEN STOVE

"I recently moved into a house, and the kitchen stove had been kept in a spotless condition, so I want to keep it that way.

"Please let me know the best way to do this."

The most important thing is to wipe off any spills or

burnt-on food as soon as the burners have cooled, so that there is no grease or spilled food build-up.

But if it does become necessary to do a bang-up cleaning job, here's what to do:

First, place all removable parts from your stove top (grids, burner and drip trays) in your kitchen sink or bathtub, and cover them with hot water, adding about one-half cup of electric dishwasher compound and let soak overnight.

Clean the rest of the stove top with a cloth or sponge, wrung out in hot, detergent water.

Don't forget the range hood (if your stove has one).

Range hoods have filters to catch the grease in exhaust fumes, and collect dust as the fan pulls the air through the filter. Check this filter often, and clean it when necessary to keep it unplugged—and your exhaust system will run more quietly and be more efficient in its operation.

Next morning you will find the carbon and grease, which has soaked off the stove parts, floating on top of the cold water in the sink.

Scrub all parts with a stiff brush, to remove any carbon, grease or film which did not soak off.

Drain sink, or bathtub, and refill with hot sudsy water. Finish the cleaning job with a sponge, then dry the parts so they will not drip on the floor when you carry them back to your nice, clean stove.

OVEN CLEANING

Here is another new idea. I can't tell you why or how this works . . . but it does!

When we clean our ovens and broilers, no matter what method we use, there is always that little wiggly rackholder gadget along the sides of it. How do we get the grease spatters off?

Some of these sides cannot be removed and soaked in your bathtub with electric dishwasher compounds like the grates and other removable parts. Soap-filled pads just do not get completely up into these grooves, do they?

I have learned, after testing many, many times, a new way to do this!

Buy some electric dishwasher compound that is ordinarily used to wash dishes in an electric dishwasher.

Wet a paper napkin or paper towel under your water faucet and shake off the water. Sprinkle the paper napkin with the dishwasher compound! Sprinkle it just as if you were using salt. The granules will adhere to the wet paper napkin or towel.

Now, the secret is to take this wet, sprinkled paper napkin and, holding it against the sides of those grooves, press the sprinkled side into the grooves with your fingers.

Within 20 minutes (and if you leave it there two hours it doesn't make any difference, so long as the paper napkin doesn't dry out), you can remove that paper napkin and it will be as black as tar!

All accumulated carbon in those little grooves will be dissolved.

Do not waste this napkin you have treated. After you remove it, use it to wipe those little, dirty grooves.

Use this same napkin and turn it over to the other side to rub-a-dub-dub until you get most of the soil off.

Then, before using any kind of rinse water, just take a soap-filled pad and wipe the grooves. Naturally, you can rinse this later with a light vinegar-water solution.

Gals, this is the only way I know of to get them really clean!

ALUMINUM UTENSILS

We have so many questions regarding the care of aluminum utensils, as to what causes warping, discoloration, etc., that I am going to give you some advice which we received from the research director of an aluminum company:

"To remove discoloration caused by minerals present in foods and some water, boil a solution of either two tablespoons of vinegar or two tablespoons of cream of tartar per quart of water in a pan 10 to 15 minutes. Water discoloration may be avoided by water conditioning.

"If food should burn in an aluminum utensil, fill pan with warm water, boil a few minutes, then scrape loose with a wooden clothespin or small stick. (Never use a knife or other metallic scraper which will scratch or gouge the aluminum. Pan then may be scoured with cleanser, steel wool and soap, or a soap-filled scouring pad.

"To avoid warping, do NOT overheat the utensil. If a gas range is used, tip of flame should just touch the bottom of pan, NEVER flare up around the sides. If an electric range is used, use high heat only a few minutes, then switch to medium. Once food is brought to cooking temperature, heat may be reduced to low."

WAXING FLOORS

"For the mothers who must wax their kitchen and bathroom floors to say nothing of the rest of the house . . . I would like to tell you my method.

"When I use liquid wax I always dilute it with two parts of very hot water. The hot water thins the wax down and not only makes it go on easier, but it dries three times as fast. I notice also that I do not get a build-up when using this method.

137

"The hot water also seems to melt the wax already on the floor and fill up those little scratches which children's shoes and the heels of women's shoes make."

ASPHALT TILE

"I am the mother of four little boys.

"I know you will understand when I say we have spots on our asphalt tile in the bathroom.

"Have you ever found anything that will remove these spots? I have tried everything. . . .

Go to your kitchen cabinet and get some liquid (not solid) vegetable oil (brand makes no difference), and put a dab of it on a piece of tissue. Rub that white spot on your asphalt tile briskly for a minute or so.

Go on with your regular work and forget about the spot for a few hours.

Come back and do the same thing over again. Remember to rub it hard and fast, as the friction from rubbing will lend heat to the white mark.

If they are old stains, it may take several applications.

Now, you will find your asphalt floor will have all the color brought back to it, and you will want to do the whole floor with the vegetable oil.

DON'T!

This procedure is to be applied only where there are white stains on asphalt.

Stains are often caused on asphalt tile in the kitchen when we spill vinegar and certain foods on it.

The oil does not take the place of waxes, etc. Besides —it's not good for the tile, but is the only thing I know of that will help restore the color to the spots on your floor.

So, just use it on those stains.

WASHING WINDOWS

Ever tried washing your windows with old-fashioned cornstarch? It's the greatest. And so inexpensive.

Put a half-gallon of warm water in a plastic waste basket and add one-fourth cup of cornstarch and stir it up. Then just wash away. They can be wiped with a squeegee or newspapers.

I find this mixture not only cuts the dirt faster but the windows shine like mad. Seem to stay clean longer too.

Don't ever wash windows on the side of the house that the sun is shining on. This causes them to streak real easy. Besides . . . why work in the sun?

If you wipe them up and down on the inside and cross-ways on the outside and then have a streak you'll know which side its on.

TAKE THE WORK OUT OF WOODWORK

Everybody has been asking me how they should WASH WOODWORK.

Heavens to Betsy! There are fifty million cleaners on the market! And each of us has different kinds of wood and paints on the woodwork throughout our homes.

But here's how I have done it for years: Don't faint! It's kerosene! Yeah!

Put about a gallon of warm water in a plastic waste-basket (or something!) and add a half cup of kerosene (bought at most filling stations for about 20 to 25 cents a gallon . . . real cheap, I'd say).

The kerosene will float on top of that warm water.

Dip an old washrag or piece of bath towel in this, wring it out and rub away—wow, what a clean job you have in a jiffy.

I have been told by painters that this cannot hurt woodwork painted with ENAMEL. In fact, they say it helps preserve it.

This does not have to be rinsed, and leaves a glossy coat on the woodwork and doors. It's also wonderful on painted metal cabinets in your kitchen.

Remember, don't try to use this with a sponge. Just use that old washrag, towel, or piece of discarded T-shirt. Works like magic.

So, gals, next time you drive into a filling station, buy some kerosene. You don't have to buy a whole gallon, but I bet you will go back soon and buy it by the gallon! Imagine finding something that works so well and is so cheap!

PAMPERED PATINA

For years I have used DUSTCLOTHS and many kinds of waxes, oils and furniture polishes, and guess what I just learned?

When you pour the polish either on the table or on the dustcloth (even if your dustcloth is presaturated), take a few facial tissues and before you start dusting put them under your dusting cloth. Just watch how much that tissue (which costs you practically nothing) absorbs the dust and soil! Gals, put it on EITHER or BOTH sides of your dusting cloth and then just mop away.

The greatest thing about this is that when you put the tissue on the bottom of the cloth and then wipe your table, the oil or wax will soak through the tissue while the soil adheres to your throw-away tissue. The good oil or wax which has been put in your cloth can be used over and over again.

By using this method, your dustcloth will stay cleaner much longer and you're saved the chore of shaking it out.

OUT, OUT, STUBBORN DIRT

From Louisiana: "Many times I had been intending to buy a RADIATOR BRUSH, but kept forgetting. In desperation, I took the long-handled brush that my husband uses to clean the snow off the car.

"It worked wonderfully! It is narrow and slides in behind the radiators and cleans the mopboards.

"It also cleans under my stove, washer and dryer."

From Washington, D.C.: "Whenever I clean and polish my furniture (especially when I use an oily-type polish), I stuff my POLISHING CLOTH down inside an old nylon stocking.

This method leaves no lint from the polishing cloth on my beautiful furniture."

This works beautifully! Not only did it leave no lint, but I found that it kept my polishing cloth cleaner, too. When the stocking became soiled, I discarded it (no drain on the budget) and used another.

I found, too, that if I cut off the foot of the stocking and tie a knot in the cut end of the leg part, it makes a better-sized cloth to work with.

From New Jersey: "Put an old sock on a BOTTLE OF FURNITURE POLISH or wax so that when the bottle is set down on anything, it won't leave a mark or scratch. The sock also catches any polish that might run down the sides of the bottle and prevents the bottle from slipping out of your hands."

"Take the sponge off your SPONGE MOP, soak it in water (so that it is maximum size), wrap the sponge in a piece of nylon net, tuck it in at the corners neatly and put it back on your mop!

"Now you can really get those stubborn spots off your floors with no effort at all! Just watch those spills and marks disappear.

"I have found that if I carry a RUBBER ERASER around in my cleaning basket I can easily remove Junior's works of art from many things around the house.

LOVE THAT VINEGAR

From Indiana: "I clean my PLASTIC BATHROOM TILE with vinegar and water, then dry and polish it with a bath towel. It looks like a mirror.

"I wash my painted kitchen cabinets, then rinse with warm vinegar water and polish with a towel. There are absolutely no streaks, either. What a time-saver that vinegar is!"

"'When you have mopped a floor and allowed it to dry, do you notice a film that dulls the luster on your linoleum or tile? If so, pour a cup of vinegar into a pail of water and go over the floor again.

"You'd be surprised how nicely the floor will shine."

TRY PROTECTIVE FILMS

"If you paste-wax the CHROME FIXTURES in your shower stall or bathtub, the chrome will stay spot-free. The water beads beautifully, rolls off, and will not streak.

"This is especially good for those who live in hard-water

areas, or have lots of soap film in their shower stalls or bathtubs."

"When working around the house, we all get our hands dirty with grease, paint, and what have you.

"TO CLEAN MY HANDS, I take a few drops of baby oil, massage my hands well with the oil, wipe with a dry cloth, then wash with my favorite soap and water."

You are so right! I have always found if you put a few drops of baby oil on your hands before beginning the chore, the paint, etc., comes off twice as easily when you rub them with a bath towel after applying a few more drops.

"I always keep my DUSTPAN WAXED, as the dirt will slide off it much more easily than from an unwaxed one."

"When WAXING FLOORS, I always wax the feet of the chairs and the runners of the rockers so they won't mar my floor when they are moved about. Waxing jobs last longer this way."

CLEANING EASYS

"ELECTRIC CORDS are a bother when dusting or vacuuming . . . besides making it easy to pull over a lamp or whatever.

"I screw a cup hook in the back of my dressers, desk, buffet, etc., then put the excess cord over the hook. Not only are the cords out of my way and off the floor, but appearances are better because less of the cord shows underneath the furniture."

During the summer months keep clear plastic over hot air registers. This keeps the residue out of the ducts and filters.

Those SPONGE MITTS you slip over your hand to wash the car can be used in the house, too!

They are perfect in the bathroom to scrub the tub or a small floor space. Good in the kitchen, also for washing down areas such as cabinets, stove, refrigerator.

They cover large surfaces quickly, and have the added attraction of protecting your hands.

Here's another glove trick for quickie cleaning. It's a fast and easy way TO POLISH SILVERWARE. I put on rubber gloves, dip a couple of fingers in paste-type polish, and rub away.

When my gloves get black, I rinse them under running water, and start over again.

This way, I can clean and polish my silver beautifully, with no cloth to get messy and dirty, and my hands and fingernails stay nice and clean, too.

"I am a busy mother and active in the community.

"When I have A MESSY JOB to do in the house, I wrap a paper towel around the telephone receiver, and secure it with a rubber band.

"Then, if I get any calls, and my hands are wet or dirty, I save a towel, time, and energy (no second cleaning job on the phone)."

"I have floor-length drapes in all my rooms, and before I wash my floors and wax them, I draw my drapes all the way back, fold the bottoms up a bit and stick the loose bottoms into a large brown grocery sack to prevent their getting splashed or soiled!

"The drapery holds the bag off the floor and the sacks hold the drapery out of the way of my broom, mop, water, etc.

"If your drapes are very heavy, use a pin to hold the sack in place. Then, instead of having to brush them when the job is finished, I just pop them out of the bag."

"I find a child's skateboard fine to kneel on and scoot around the room for low dusting and wiping up floors."

STICKY TRICKS

A question was put to me by a young mother in Washington. She explained:

"With several small children in the house, I continually find chewing gum stuck to their hair . . . which is an awful problem. Please tell me how to deal with this sticky mess!"

I couldn't send her a magic wand, but I did have a procedure that works.

FOR REMOVING CHEWING GUM from children's hair: Use an ice cube first and pick out as much as possible. Then apply egg white or peanut butter. This will soften the gum. Wipe hair between fingers using a facial tissue or cloth.

From Oregon: "Did you know that baby oil will remove ADHESIVE TAPE STUCK TO THE SKIN? Just saturate a piece of cotton with it and rub. The tape comes right off and doesn't burn the skin. It smells good, too."

STAINS AWAY

From Vermont: "When we had our house painted white this year, my two-year-old decided to wash his hands in the paint bucket. When I tried to clean his hands, both of us wound up with white hands!

"His young skin was so sensitive I didn't want to use turpentine on it. Our painter told us to use salad oil or margarine.

145

"We poured oil on our hands and used old pieces of cloth to WIPE OFF THE PAINT. It worked like magic."

From Minnesota: "For those who still like to use a regular fountain pen to write with, but are often annoyed by INK STAINS on the fingers, I suggest that they wet the tip of the head of a safety match, and apply it to the stain. The stain will disappear like magic."

LINENS

"What causes small holes in my linens? Some of them are less than two months old."

We have taken this up with the President of the Home Laundry Manufacturers' Association. He has had home economists do research on this and here is the answer so far as we know:

The first reaction is that the customer has misused bleach. If bleach has been used correctly a further explanation is difficult.

They enclosed such technical data that I will try to simplify it for you as follows:

Household bleaches used full strength for cleaning purposes can seriously weaken the fibers in a cleaning cloth or dishrag, unless the bleach is thoroughly rinsed out. Furthermore, other fabrics that come in contact with the cleaning cloth can also be damaged.

Further damage to other fabrics may result from contact with the unrinsed cleaning cloth. For example, if you pour pure household bleach on your dishcloth for bleaching your sink, then drop it into a laundry hamper or a laundry bag, any cellulose fabric that comes in contact with this cleaning cloth will be weakened by the remaining bleach.

This cloth may stay in your laundry hamper for a few days. It is impossible to see what damage it has done to other fibers which have been in contact with the cleaning cloth until they are washed! Then when the linen is washed the weak fibers in your sheets will crumple and float away leaving little holes and tiny tears. Your washcloth will have more damage but this is immaterial to you as it only costs a few cents. And your sheets are quite expensive.

Check up on how you use your bleach and see if you are following the directions on the bottle or box, whether it is liquid or dry bleach.

Another thing that causes holes in laundry is that you just might happen to have a rough spot in either your washing machine or the drier, which will cause snagging and damage too. Never overload your machine.

This is valuable information we have received from the Home Laundry Manufacturers' Association and we are most grateful for it.

CANDLE DRIPPINGS

To get rid of the candle wax you all get from candle drippings on clothing, linens and carpets.

ON CARPETS:

Take a spoon and scrape off as much as possible. Then go grab that box of facial tissues. If you don't have any, use WHITE paper napkins. Lay three or four thicknesses on top of the spilled wax and using your iron set on SYNTHETIC or MEDIUM, just iron away. As soon as the grease appears on the paper, remove it IMMEDIATELY (so that you won't iron it right back into the rug). Replace with fresh tissues. Repeat process until napkin no longer absorbs any grease.

A safe dry-cleaning fluid might be effective in many cases. However, it should be used sparingly to avoid damage to the latex backing which so many rugs have today. But it is doubtful that any will be needed if the above method is used.

ON TABLES:

They are probably ruined, as I know you have removed the wax and finish when the hot wax hit it. However, let's do the best we can.

Cover the spot with foil! Then lay a hot washrag on top. This will melt the wax beautifully and make it easy to remove. Most times it will just roll off like bubble gum.

Lighter fluid (read cautions) may be necessary, but this will remove the waxes on your table and it will, natch, have to be rewaxed.

DON'T dig at it with a table knife or spoon. Use your pancake turner! It has a flat edge that won't make indentations in your table top. Only use this if it is a big glob. If you have small spots, use your fingernail.

ON YOUR COTTON CLOTHING AND TABLECLOTHS:

Rub material with an ice cube or freeze in your deep freezer until the wax is hard. Most of it will flick off with your fingernail. Remove as much wax as possible. Rub cloth between the hands while still cold. More will come out! Brush off excess particles.

Place white paper napkins or facial tissues above and beneath the waxed spot and iron with a warm iron. When paper napkin shows grease spot, remove immediately and replace with fresh napkins. When no more spots appear on napkin, wash as usual or clean with a safe dry-cleaning fluid.

ON CANDELABRA:

Just run hot water until the wax melts! Be sure that you do not wet felt if any happens to be on the bottom. Polish as usual.

And for heaven's sake, next time your lights go out, tear off a piece of foil and place under the candle holder BEFORE lighting them! Or if you have no holders, use a saucer or one of those throw-away pie tins.

WASH FEATHER DUSTER

"Can you wash a feather duster? Mine leaves more marks than a pencil carried by any of my grandchildren!"

The reason your feather duster leaves marks is probably that you have used it on things you have waxed and also for things on which you have used an oil rag. Oil and waxes don't mix!

Wash the duster but don't dare throw it in a washing machine.

Here's how I wash mine:

Put a little detergent in the washbasin, then fill the basin with hot water.

Wave the duster over and then DOWN into this suds. . . .

Watch that water get black as coal. Rinse the feathers under the COLD water faucet until the water is clear.

It will look like you have a wet chicken, and you will think that old feather duster is ruined, but it won't be.

Fix another basin of suds. Do the same thing again.

Then, to get your bottle of vinegar. Put a blub-blub from the bottle in your basin. (That's about a fourth of a cup.)

Fill it with warm water and rinse away!

Shake that old feather duster over your bathtub to get excess water out. (It will now look like a wet, sick hen.)

Stand it on end (with the featherside UP) or hang on your clothesline and next morning you will wonder where all those delightful feathery feathers came from! And why you didn't wash the duster every week or so. . . .

House Beautiful

We all like our homes to be as nice as possible, and of course keeping them neat and clean is the first requisite. Then, too, you've got to keep a sharp eye out for unsightliness. If the edge of the rug starts to unravel, get right on it with a needle and thread. If the throw cushions look like they've seen better days, be daring and get a fresh batch at the next sale that comes along.

In the meantime, keep adding those touches that give a home charm and comfort. You can do it economically, too.

You'll notice that some of the following hints are for those who try to be over-meticulous. It's possible to kill something "with kindness"!

Do you know anyone who doesn't make a beeline to a comfy chair covered in a cheery fabric? Slipcovers are one of the most important elements in the "house beautiful." They not only protect furniture, but they also change the appearance of a room.

I have made SLIPCOVERS for my furniture for years, using slipcover material, sailcloth, and upholstery material. The latter was thick, so it protected the material of the furniture and didn't look as much like a slipcover . . . but it had to be dry cleaned, and that's expensive.

The last time I needed new slipcovers I thought, "Why not toss those old ideas about the 'usual' fabrics right out the window?"

Then it dawned on me how inexpensive, attractive and practical corduroy would be. Besides, it's soft and cuddly. It comes in different widths, a myriad of colors and patterns, and either wide, narrow or variegated wale (that's the width of those ridges).

I bought 45-inch width material, and used it CROSSWISE, and I didn't waste nearly as much material, because the pieces I cut off the selvage (when I cut out the cushion covers) were perfect for making the dust ruffle around the bottom of the cover, inserts around the cushions, and protectors for the arm rests.

All pieces of the corduroy should go the same way— either up or down or sideways—otherwise some of the pieces will look lighter than the rest, almost as if they had faded. It doesn't really make any difference whether the ribs go north or south, but all should point in the same direction.

Another good thing about using the material crosswise is that the cushions don't scoot out of the seat of the couch or chairs. The nap of the corduroy, turned crosswise, prevents this.

You would be surprised how easy it is to sew with, and on, corduroy. It doesn't ravel badly, like so many other materials I have used for slipcovering.

And, if you don't know how to sew too well, do what I did . . . I used cotton fringe (bought at dime or department store—just be sure it's washable) instead of cording. The fringe literally hides your mistakes if the seams aren't absolutely straight!

When the covers became soiled, I cleaned part of them in a do-it-yourself dry cleaning machine, and washed the others, just brushing them with a stiff brush after putting them back on. With both methods, the covers came out fluffy and beautiful and did not have to be ironed.

You might think corduroy would be hot in summer, but t'ain't so! And in the winter it looks warm and cozy.

The next time you slipcover a chair or couch, how about trying corduroy? I think you'll like it as much as I do.

FABRIC-A-DABRA

Stop, look, and listen! It's nylon net again, this time beautifying your dining table at a very, very, low cost. A friend of mine sent me the most beautiful nylon net TABLE-CLOTH that she made from two and one-half yards of net. (*Good* net; she watches her bargains and picked the best bolt on the table.)

She makes the cloths for practically nothing. Figure: Two and one-half yards of net costs you less than a dollar. Plus the fact that this net is seventy-two inches wide . . . that's a real bargain.

She bought some lace to edge it with. If you make a cloth two and one-half yards long, it will take nine yards of lace to go around the edge of the cloth. Do not hem the edge of the net before sewing the lace on. Just machine stitch the lace on the edge.

BUT . . . My friend was sharp. She bought inexpensive NYLON lace. This way when she washes the cloth, NOTHING has to be ironed!

Being the smartie-pie she is, she also bought some WIDE lace with pretty little medallions in it. She took her scissors and cut these flowers out and hand-stitched them on all four corners and stitched a few in the middle of the cloth. This was not expensive. Check and compare your prices, gals. It only takes about one-half yard of the wide lace. Pick some with pretty designs that are easy to cut out.

If you use white net, it is very attractive over a pastel tablecloth or sheet. Red or green net is very festive for the Christmas holidays, bronze over white for Thanksgiving, pure white for a bridal party, etc. And this cloth is lovely when used on a bare, highly polished table.

You can also make individual place mats of the net and trim them the same way as the tablecloth.

Most of us can't afford tablecloths for every special occasion, and the net is so inexpensive that we can have a larger variety of colors suitable for the season or the event.

The cloths and mats wash beautifully and do not require ironing.

What a fabulous idea for wedding gifts, etc. Imagine getting a set of beautiful place mats!

SOME FACTS ON FURNISHINGS

From New York: "Have just learned an expensive lesson . . . not long ago, I had my dining room set, and a living room chair, done over in antique white LACQUER FINISH.

"Now, says me to m'self, I'm not going to be yelling at

our poor little dog and cat to keep off the furniture; I'll just get some plastic covers and when company comes, yank the covers off and chuck 'cm behind the couch. Then the furniture will always look like new.

"Well, this worked out fine for a while, 'til one day I yanked and woops—along came the paint in spots and ridges on the plastic!

"Well, after I calmed down, I called the furniture man who had done the work. My tears ran down as I wailed, and he said, 'My gosh woman, don't you know that you NEVER let plastic come in contact with paint or lacquer? Never but NEVER put a plastic purse or wallet on a finished surface or the same thing could happen.'

"It takes time for this chemical action to happen, so it may not happen the first time, or even the second, and MAYBE not with every kind of plastic. And it may take time for it to work through a coat of wax, but believe me, Heloise, it's not worth taking the chance."

From Connecticut: "We have just purchased two new LAMPSHADES for the living room.

"Is it all right for me to leave the cellophane wrapping on them so they will stay clean longer?"

No, it *isn't* a good idea to leave the cellophane protector on lampshades, and here's why: The heat from the lamp bulb will cause the cellophane to shrink and that may pull your lampshades out of shape. Besides, it may cause streaks on your beautiful shades. It is better to remove the cellophane before you use the shades.

From Oklahoma: "Did you know that rust spots on painted WROUGHT-IRON FURNITURE can be removed by using oily furniture polish, such as lemon oil?

"I find this also helps eliminate the possibility of future rust."

From Georgia: "A small picnic table (the type with benches attached), when painted or stained, makes ideal KITCHEN FURNITURE for a family. Quite inexpensive, too."

CLEAR PLASTIC CHAIR COVERS

"Do you know what can be done in a jiffy with a swatch of leftover drapery material, or any other fabric?

"I simply press transparent adhesive-backed plastic paper to the TOP side of the material, smooth it carefully *with my hand, not an iron* . . .

"No hemming is necessary, and you can cut the completed job with pinking shears into any shape you prefer. This makes handy, easy-to-clean table runners, doilies for lamp bases, etc."

Another idea:

Next time you cover your dining room chairs, buy some extra material, and make yourself some place mats for your dining room table! Then all would match. With the swipe of a damp sponge, they could be cleaned in a jiffy.

If your child is prone to dropping food on your upholstered dining room chairs, try using this method on them.

Also . . . the transparent plastic does not look shiny. It is hardly noticeable.

This idea could certainly be utilized for those of you who have polished cotton kitchen curtains and want to cover your breakfast or dining room chairs to match. Heretofore, polished cotton was quite impractical to cover chairs. But, not any more!

Next time you make new kitchen curtains, buy extra

yardage to cover your chairs and to make some place mats for your table.

The transparent plastic can usually be bought at department and dime stores.

Remember . . . don't cover the bottom of table mats with plastic and put it on a beautiful table because it might take the finish off. Only cover the top.

FLIRTIN' WITH CURTAINS

DRAPERIES are so expensive that we like to think they'll last forever. They won't, but they can be made to last longer. Here's how.

When you buy unlined pinch-pleat draperies . . . never rip out the pinch-pleats and reline them. Do this:

Use bed sheets, tinted or white, for the lining, but do not sew them to the new curtains ANYWHERE under ANY circumstances.

Instead, leave those beautiful new curtains right there on the traverse rod, hanging in all their glory, and literally duplicate them, pinch-pleats, length, width and all . . . with sheets.

Then buy another set of drapery pins and put them in the pleats of the "sheet" curtains. Then proceed to hang these sheet curtains right behind the beautiful drapes . . . the seams of each set of curtains facing each other and the right side of the sheet pinch-pleats toward the window.

This really works. The best part of this procedure is that when the lining gets soiled (and it always does first), it can be taken down and washed.

Have the other curtains dry cleaned if you wish (and we all know that dry cleaning for unlined drapes is far cheaper than for lined ones).

One need not buy extra rods at all this way, only the

curtain hooks, as the little tab of the traverse rod will easily hold the two sets of curtains.

When hanging the separate lining to the original curtain, work the folds of the lining (or sheet) so that they conform with those of the real curtain itself. They will "train" as you open and close your drapes . . . and the two sets will stay together just as if they were made at the same time.

From Nevada: "The DRAPES on the sunny side of the living room were always becoming sun-streaked.

"The last time I made new ones, I bought material which had no up-and-down design and put hems of the same width in both the top and the bottom of the drapes.

"Every couple of months, I take the drapes off the rods and hang them upside down. This way they fade more evenly, so it is less noticeable."

From Quebec: "People would not have to have their DRAPERIES cleaned so often if they would just take them down, remove the pins, put the drapes in the dryer, and let them tumble without heat.

"This removes most of the dust that ordinarily causes rotting of draperies."

From North Carolina: "When the tapes and cords on my VENETIAN BLINDS get dingy and yellow-looking, I thin white shoe polish with water and apply it with a damp washcloth. The polish must be made very thin because it usually dries whiter than white and we do not want a buildup on the tape."

From Missouri: "SHOWER CURTAIN dingy and discolored after long use?

158

"Buy a good shower curtain, hang on SAME hooks as old one, leaving new curtain hanging on the outside of the tub.

"Or, buy an inexpensive one for inside the tub and a more expensive, pretty one for hanging on the outside. The one you want company to see remains in perfect condition."

FROSTING WINDOWS

"For those who live close to a neighbor and want to frost a front door, bathroom window or kitchen window, here is the method I have tried and found most satisfactory:

"I dissolve one tablespoon of epsom salts in a small amount of beer and apply the mixture with a brush to the inside of my windowpanes. It is the best frosting I have ever seen.

"I used one cup of beer, adding the epsom salts to suit myself. (I used four heaping tablespoonsful.)

"I applied the mixture with a 2″ paint brush. It not only covered the window, but looked like Jack Frost himself! It dries beautifully, lasts a long time, and when washed off is easily reapplied. It's amazing how it crystallizes."

THE BEAUTY OF SILVER

Many a bride blessed with gifts of STERLING SILVER FLATWARE sometimes hesitates to use her new treasure simply because she thinks it should be saved for special occasions.

This couldn't be farther from the truth!

The remarkable and unique quality of sterling silver, which sets it apart from almost all other household possessions, is that it actually improves with use.

The best care you can give your sterling is to use it—

not just for Sundays, or for parties, or for special dinners, but every day of your life.

Constant use gives sterling a patina it never achieves when locked away in the darkness of a chest. Patina consists of thousands of tiny lines which, while almost invisible, produce the soft, mellow surface that makes very old silver so lovely.

You can wash sterling either by hand or in an automatic dishwasher.

Wash it immediately after use in hot soapy water and rinse it in clear, hot water. Wipe it with a soft cloth after rinsing or when the dishwasher's cycle is completed, for air-drying causes almost all metals to water spot.

The Sterling Silversmiths of America give the following recommendations for occasional beauty treatments for your sterling:

1. Always use a polish that's specified for silver. All-purpose metal polishes are usually too harsh for silver and may damage the surface.
2. Polish with long, horizontal strokes rather than rubbing with a circular motion. Use restraint in polishing heavily ornamented areas. The dark oxidation in the crevices gives depth to the design and adds to its beauty.

Several new silver polishes are made specifically to retard the formation of tarnish, and are particularly good for sterling hollowware pieces kept on display. Effectiveness of these polishes depends to a great extent on atmospheric conditions.

Store silver away from the air. You can keep it in a silver chest, or wrap it in tarnish-preventing cloth, or place it in a drawer lined with the same cloth.

Do NOT store silver with rubber-backed place mats or

secure roll-up bags with rubber bands. This will cause tarnishing, since rubber contains sulphur.

Remember, though—silver is to USE. It thrives on a busy life, and will grow more beautiful through the years.

FOR INVITING KITCHENS

Those of you who paper your own KITCHENS or have them papered . . . always buy an extra roll (you can also save the scraps after papering) and keep it on hand to cover the shelves. It matches your walls and is darling.

After helping a friend paper her kitchen last week, we covered all the shelves and the insides of the drawers to match. We covered the paper in the drawers with plastic so that she can wipe them with a damp sponge.

On the shelves, we put waxed paper over the wallpaper. It was cheaper and the paper just happened to fit the shelves. We used pinking scissors to make an edge.

When a cabinet is opened or a drawer is pulled out, everything matches.

My friend then went out and bought an extra roll of paper just to have on hand when it becomes necessary to replace the shelf and drawer liners.

Wallpaper is not only attractive and practical, but is cheaper than most shelf paper.

HOUSEHOLD HIGHLIGHTS

When you build a CENTERPIECE OF FRUIT for your table, use a grapefruit or two first. This forms a mound.

Before you place your apples on it, polish them with a thin coat of vegetable oil and rub well with paper napkins. This will make them shine! And a good vegetable oil will not ruin the taste.

I always put lemons, limes, oranges, a banana or two and some grapes on top.

This is not a waste of money because the fruit can be eaten later or used for fruit salads, etc.

From Nevada: "To KEEP PICTURES STRAIGHT on the wall, I wrap a piece of masking tape around my index finger a few times (sticky side out), making a small ring. Then I put the tape on the back of the frame near the bottom and press it against the wall.

"The picture will stick to the wall and won't have to be straightened every time it is dusted. The masking tape is easy to remove from the wall and leaves no mark on the paint."

From Illinois: "I took my dingy WHITE CANDLES from the candlesticks and was ready to toss them out, but decided to try washing them in detergent and not-too-warm water. They look like new again. Try it!"

From Alaska: "Here is an idea for an inexpensive DOORKEEPER.

"I painted a large rock with gold paint and it looks like we Alaskans are so rich that we can prop doors open with king-size gold nuggets!"

From New Mexico: "Here's an idea for using cinder blocks as DOORSTOPS.

"I covered the bottom of a block with masking tape to protect the floor. Then I stuffed leftover plastic foam into the holes in the block and sprayed it with gold paint. When it was dry, I inserted artificial flowers into the foam.

"This doorstop is pretty enough to be left out . . . even when not stopping a door!"

WISE WAYS FOR WATERING

From Pennsylvania: "I have many POTTED PLANTS in my house but have always found it a messy job to keep them watered.

"Finally I hit upon the idea of using a plastic toothbrush holder!

"Cut off both ends of the plastic tube. Place one end of the tube in the soil in the flowerpot and fill it with water about once a week (depending on the size of the plant).

"This saves a great deal of time and avoids wet table tops."

I tried it. I inserted the tube about one inch deep in the soil. The water will drain slowly into the dirt. Wet the soil thoroughly before trying to insert the tube. Push the tube into the soil, pull the tube out and blow the mud from the end of it back into the pot. Insert the empty tube again. Then fill it with water. That's all there is to it.

Fantastic. I also put plant food into the tube before putting water in it, when my plants need extra feeding. Any small plastic tube will do.

From New York: "Here's a dandy idea for WATERING HOUSEPLANTS while you are away for a short while. Cut a strip of cloth two inches wide and two feet long. Put one end of the strip in a pail of water which is set higher than the plant, and bury the other end of the strip in the soil of the plant. This is good for about a week. The water will gently seep down into the pot."

And here's another approach to the same problem.

From South Carolina: "Before going away for a week, I covered my HOUSEPLANTS with plastic bags, after watering the plants well.

"The moisture rises and condenses inside the bags, then falls back on the plants.

"When I returned home, all of the plants were fresh and perky.

"The tomato seeds I had planted before leaving, and also covered with a plastic bag, had sprouted nicely."

A hint for WATERING SMALL PLANTS: Use an empty plastic catsup or mustard squeeze-type container partly filled with water. As the water squirts in a stream, there is no chance of overflowing or drowning the plant.

From Georgia: "If people will cover the tops of the FLOWER BOXES which contain soil and flowers with a half inch of gravel, it will keep the soil from splashing when watering, and drying out."

POT-POURRI

From Utah: "Instead of just using a rock or a piece of broken clay pot over the hole in your FLOWERPOT, try putting a swatch of cotton material over the hole before placing the rock in the pot!

"This little piece of material keeps the soil from running out after each watering."

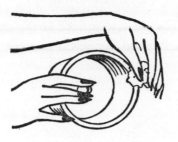

Another good suggestion when TRANSPLANTING plants to larger pots is to cut a piece of sponge about one inch thick to fit the bottom of the new pot.

The sponge not only keeps the dirt from sifting through the hole, but also holds the moisture.

POT LUCK

From Florida: "To keep plants from falling or being blown off the ledge on our porch, I hammered a long, thin nail into the ledge, and fit the hole of the flowerpot over the nail. This trick keeps the PLANTS ON THE PORCH quite secure."

From New Jersey: "I display my PLANTS ON AN OUTSIDE WINDOW sill without any danger of their tipping or falling by attaching a curtain rod to the window frame so that the rod runs across at a level just above the center of the pots."

ROOMS OF BLOOMS

Most of our beloved INDOOR PLANTS, ivy, philodendron and other nonflowering houseplants, benefit from an occasional shower. This removes the accumulated dust from the leaves and thoroughly wets the support pole on which the plant grows.

I water my plants in our bathtub under a gentle shower of cool water. (If the potted plant is real small, I sometimes use the spray hose in the kitchen sink.) But there is a catch to watering and washing the leaves of a plant like this . . . overflowing and overwatering could result.

I first place the flowerpot in a big piece of soft plastic (which I have saved from the dry cleaner's) and draw the plastic up and around the pot, covering the soil to keep it from washing away while under the shower. Then I pull it tight around the stems of the plant, tying it with string, and shower away!

The water washes all the dust off the leaves without drowning the plant.

If you have trouble getting long-stemmed flowers to stand up straight in WIDEMOUTHED VASES, try nylon net!

I put the flowers in the vase first, then lightly tuck the nylon net down into the vase, all the way around the inside, until the flowers are braced into the desired position.

The nylon net does not absorb the water and collapse like paper towels or cloth. It is firm yet pliable, stays in whatever position I place it, and doesn't tear the stems.

From West Virginia: "I have found that the most attractive and inexpensive SUPPORT FOR TALL PHILODEN-

DRONS and similar plants is an adjustable, brass-colored curtain rod (straight type). It can grow with the plant and costs less than 50 cents.

"Since many of us have brass accents in our furnishings, this makes an added room decoration."

GROW 'EM YOURSELF

From Iowa: "When friends ask the name of my exotic-looking HOUSEPLANTS, it's fun to explain that they are avocado trees raised from seeds.

"Whenever I splurge on an avocado pear, I save the large, stone-type seed, and plant it in at least an eight-inch pot of soil mixed with peat moss or leaf mold.

"The only trick is to keep it very moist. Covering the pot with a sheet of plastic wrap promotes a greenhouse atmosphere."

From Colorado: "For those who love green things: Cut about one inch off the big end of a carrot and place it in a shallow container in some water, and it will make a LOVELY FERN. Just watch it grow!

"I cut off the top of a fresh pineapple and set it in a pot of water and it, too, makes a lovely houseplant!"

From Florida: "Plastic LEMON- AND LIME-JUICE CON-
TAINERS make cute vases if the tops are cut off. They're
flat on the bottom, so they won't tip.

"I fill the plastic container with soil, and put a tiny
plant in it. Violets, pansies and other short-stemmed flowers
are also lovely in them. It is small enough to set on the
window sill and is cheerful-looking and attractive."

OUTDOOR DECOR

Bugs are the bane of outdoor living. One enterprising
lady from New York told how her family solved that problem . . . cheaply.

"We made a screened-in, portable OUTDOOR ROOM, using
sixteen yards of nylon net (seventy-two inches wide).

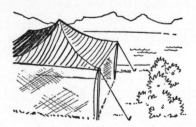

"We added a striped canvas roof, and sewed rope along
the sides of the canvas to hold it in shape. The net is sewn
to the edges of the roof. We put a pole in the middle and

used four corner posts. The posts are permanent, with hooks to hold the corners of the net and canvas. We have four extra poles to use when we go camping.

"Our 'room' is 10 x 12 feet, with a lapped-over opening at each end for doors.

"I put beanbag weights on the bottom of both sides of the door openings and this holds the doors closed. We pegged the sides down with tent pegs.

"Our portable bugless and mosquitoless room cost less than ten dollars!"

"From California: "On our patio we use metal paint buckets from the hardware store and fill them with sand to use as OUTDOOR CIGARETTE TRAYS.

"If a piece of wire screening is placed about an inch under the sand it makes it easy to remove the used cigarettes. Paint the outside of the small buckets and decorate them any way you wish.

"These are ideal for cigarette butts as the breezes do not scatter ashes. And the buckets cost very little."

Handy Manners

I wonder how many men realize what good handymen their wives (usually) are. Most gals would rather not present their husbands with umpteen little jobs to do on their days off if they have the time and ability to do these tasks themselves while hubby is at work. And besides, this gives wives the delicious satisfaction of having accomplished something outside of the routine of washing, ironing, mending, etc.

So here are some time- and money-saving tips to help spur on you Helpmate Handymen. Amaze your family by "doing it yourself."

TAKE IT FROM THE PAINTING PROS

From Connecticut: "Painters spend a lot of time and patience tracing a one-sixteenth-inch MARGIN AROUND THE

GLASS ON WOOD SASHES to cover the putty so that water will not seep in around the glass.

"Invariably the woman of the house comes along with a sharp razor blade and shaves the paint off, and soon the putty falls off and the sash begins to decay and rot.

"So, folks, keep razor blades off the window glass. That little thin line which we put around the window is there for a purpose. It keeps the putty in and the sash from rotting."

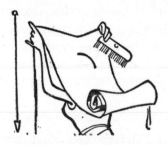

"When HANGING WALLPAPER, use a piece of string with a lead weight attached to the bottom and hang the string from the molding or ceiling line in the room.

"This weighted string acts as a guide, and helps you hang your wallpaper straight."

From Florida: "When we had our house painted I picked up a very good tip from the painter.

"Every time he opened a new can of paint, he immediately made several nail holes on the inside rim of the can. Thus, when he wiped the EXCESS PAINT off his brush, it ran right back into the can.

"If there is any paint left to store, it will not dry out because the lid fits right over the nail holes."

SPATTER MATTERS

From Washington: "Here is a hint for PAINTERS WHO WEAR GLASSES: To keep from getting drops of paint on your glasses, especially when painting overhead, cut circles of plastic wrap and smooth them over the lenses.

"The plastic will stick as though cemented, and when you are through painting, you can just peel it off. No fuss, no blots, no clean-up!"

From Arizona: "Before you start TO PAINT WINDOW FRAMES, cut strips of newspaper two inches wide.

"Dip the strips in water so they are thoroughly wet, then apply them like masking tape to the window glass . . . no more paint to scrape off the panes. And you don't even have to remove the strips, as they will fall off the glass when they are dry!

CUT THE FUSS!

"From Connecticut: "On completion of a paint job, I paint a strip from the top of the can down the side to the LEVEL OF THE PAINT left in it.

"When I again need paint I am able to see the color at a glance, and I can tell how much remains in the can.

"Each time I use paint from the can, I paint the strip on down to the new lower level.

"I am sure this will help many do-it-yourselfers."

From Utah: "I use one-pound coffee cans with plastic tops for soaking my PAINTBRUSHES.

"I cut two cross slits in the plastic lid, put the brush in the can, pour in some turpentine, and put on the lid with the brush handle sticking up through the slits.

"This way, the liquid is not likely to spill, the odors do not escape so easily, and the brush does not rest on the bottom of the can."

From Rhode Island: "If you are in the process of re-painting your home, be sure to fill some well-washed nail-polish or shoe-polish bottles with some of each color of paint you are using in the different rooms and then label them.

"Later, when a scratch appears on your wall, you are all set to do a TOUCH-UP JOB without getting the paintbrush out again! These small nail-polish and shoe-polish brushes are just the right size."

This hint is for do-it-yourself painters who use A ROLLER AND A PAN.

Line the paint pan with a solid piece of aluminum foil before you pour the paint into the pan. When you have finished painting, remove the foil and discard it. No messy paint tray to clean!

"Want a tip from a bachelor?

"If you have A CEILING TO PAINT, try a sponge wax applicator (the kind you do the floors with).

"Sure saves time and does a good job!"

FUME NOT!

A raw onion cut up and left in a room while painting makes the PAINT ODOR less potent, yet the onion odor disappears, too.

TWO WAYS TO PAINT STAIRS

You can take your choice of these two methods of doing an always bothersome job. The first may be better if stairs are quite narrow. But if there is room enough, the second way certainly seems safer.

From New York: Make it a *two-day* job. Paint even-numbered steps one day, odd-numbered ones the next . . . and you'll be able to use the stairs throughout the painting project.

From Pennsylvania: "When PAINTING STAIRS, I start by painting each step from the left side to the center.

"A few days later, after the paint has dried thoroughly,

174

I paint the other side, overlapping (or featherbrushing) the paint so that the entire step is painted.

"In this way, the unpainted side may be used while the other side is drying. With this method there is no need to paint every other step on separate days. Having to walk up and down every other step is a real invitation to an accident."

RENEW IT!

From Hawaii: "The simplest and easiest way to change worn VENETIAN BLIND CORDS is *before* they break.

"Start by cutting the bottom of the cord where the knot is tied, and tie your new cord onto this knot.

"Tie, sew, or tape the new cord to the end of the old one. After cutting the old cord, you can draw it out at the same time you are threading the new one."

We tried it, and it works!

Get your venetian blind down, look on the bottom and find the knot. Cut one side of the knot, and tie your new cord to it.

While the blind is still *hanging* in the window, *pull* the new cord, and let it run until the old one drops out of the other side. You will know then how much new cord is needed. Allow a few inches, and work from there.

It's possible to make a well-aged CEDAR CLOSET as fresh and fragrant as new. Just rent an electric belt sander and sand those cedar boards. This usually does the job. Besides, it will be nice and clean again and have a light color like it did when it was new.

Another method is to go to a hardware store and ask for oil of cedar and paint the closet. Follow directions on container.

175

SCREEN-UP TIME

From New Jersey: "I have found a wonderful way to patch HOLES IN WINDOW SCREENS . . . nylon net! Just double or triple a piece of it and sew it over the hole with a needle and thread—just as if you were patching a garment. I use gray-colored net for this and it doesn't show.

"I also stapled two thicknesses of net (one might do if it's a good grade) across the outside of the windows in our summer cabin. The net is cheaper and wider (seventy-two inches) than regular mosquito netting.

"My wife made a cover for our baby's bed and playpen by sewing two widths of the net together. This is just wonderful to keep out flies and mosquitoes. Also, it is easily tied to the legs of the bed or playpen. It can be washed in the sink, rinsed, shaken out, and used immediately."

GLASS DOORS

"Glass doors are beautiful but they can be dangerous! It is sometimes difficult to tell whether the door is open or closed, and many people have tried to walk through a closed door!

"May I suggest some precautions that can be taken to prevent accidents?

"Put attractive decals on the door at two levels . . . one high enough to be seen by an adult, and another at a child's eye level.

"Never have throw rugs in front of a glass door because there is always the possibility of slipping on the rug and falling against the door. And always be certain there are no toys or other articles near the door which might cause someone to trip.

"And never take it for granted that the door is open!"

I have been in homes where artificial butterflies (bought at the dime store) have been taped to the door and they were adorable.

Also, artificial ivy taped across the bottom of one door and up the sides *to adult eye level,* almost looks as though the ivy were growing in a planter!

If you are having a birthday party for a small child, tape balloons to the door. Not only is it attractive, but is an extra precaution because children DO run without thinking about where they are going!

GOOD OLD RUBBER

From Vermont: "There must be some older houses still around that have PULL CHAINS ON ELECTRIC LIGHTS. We have them in our basement, and do I ever appreciate the rubber fruit jar rings my husband attached to the ends of those chains, especially in the laundry.

"They are so easy to take hold of, and there is no danger of electric shocks because wet-or-damp hands *never* touch direct metal."

From Hawaii: "For a no-bruise STEPLADDER, I nailed a thin strip of sponge rubber to the front and back edges of the top step.

"This eliminates not only marks on the wall when the ladder is pushed against it, but prevents bruised shins, too."

"If you do YOUR OWN UPHOLSTERING, buy a rubber tip (which most people put on the end of a crutch or a chair) to fit the head of your hammer. Then pound away!

"You will be surprised. You will have no marks on your beautiful tacks, or if you happen to hit the woodwork around it, it won't make a mark on it."

From Illinois: "I found that renewing pencil erasers with an EMERY BOARD is easy. Roughs them up and takes the slickness away.

"I had a rubber doorstop for my back door, and it just wouldn't work any more on a windy day, so I got out the emery board, filed the doorstop, and it's good as new.

"The same treatment, applied to rubber-tipped legs on my TV lamp and ironing board, also kept them from sliding.

"Wonderful!"

If you have a leg on a piece of furniture which needs raising to balance it, try gluing a garden hose washer to the tip of the SHORT LEG. The hose washer will not show as much as a piece of paper.

HANDY NOTIONS

From a man in Denver: "Plastic lids from coffee cans can be used to COVER AN OIL CAN (quart-size) after part of the oil has been used. I use this oil for my lawn mower and use only part of it at one time. The plastic lid fits perfectly, keeps out the dirt, and prevents the oil from spilling."

"To keep a SCREW IN PLASTER WALLS, pound a small nail gently into the plaster and then remove it. Fill the hole with steel wool and then turn the screw in firmly."

To repair a BROKEN CHINA FIGURINE, why not use clear nail polish to stick the pieces together?

I tried it, and it worked. And when the mends dried, I used nail polish remover to get off the excess polish.

From New York: "Those plastic bleach bottles make wonderful SCOOPS, if they are cut correctly.

"Hold the bottle by the handle, and with a pair of scissors or a sharp knife, begin cutting one inch below the handle, and slice toward the bottom of the bottle in a curved line. The line doesn't really have to be curved; it just looks nicer.

"This scoop is wonderful when bailing water from boats, because the shape will conform to the bottom of the boat.

"Naturally, when bailing water, the top has to be screwed on, so the water won't come out the end."

From Washington: "The previous tenants of the apartment I moved into must have had at least fifty pictures on the walls. There were holes here, there and everywhere. For a quick cover-up, I took a little flour and water and made a thick paste with it.

"I plastered over all the HOLES IN THE WHITE WALLS and now I don't even need real plaster. As the flour paste began to dry, I just rubbed off the excess. The holes do not show.

"What a time, trouble, and money-saver this has been."

"When an oil can will not reach oil cups or openings inside certain machines, such as a motor behind a screen,

I force a soda straw onto the spout of the can. This can be bent to any angle for easy OILING OF HARD-TO-GET-AT PLACES."

HOW DOES MY GARDEN GROW?

From Vermont: "I always have had difficulty SAVING SEEDS of my favorite flowers until this idea hit me.

"As soon as the plants are partly dry, I pull them and put them in a big plastic bag or paper sack.

"I leave them in the bag until they are quite dried out, then shake the bag hard. All the seeds fall to the bottom of the bag.

"I then remove them, put into jars, and label them for the following year."

From Louisiana: "I have a hint for weed haters: Fill an empty squeeze bottle with WEED KILLER (be SURE to label it) then just squirt the weeds and grass in the cracks of the sidewalk and other hard-to-get-at places. Before you know it, the weeds are dead."

From New York: "I cut off the tops and bottoms of plastic bottles when they are empty. I use the remainder of the bottles to put around little plants when I am trying to get them started.

"Not only do these bottles KEEP THE PLANTS SHADED until they get their start, but if pushed down into the ground a little bit, they hold water around the roots."

From Michigan: "I have a garden at our cottage, and as we are only at the cottage for a few days at a time, weeds often get ahead of us.

"I solved this problem by spreading old newspapers out between the rows, using about three thicknesses of newspapers. After laying the papers out, spread some soil, or lay rocks on top of them to keep them from blowing away or looking too unsightly.

"I also use for this purpose any old plastics such as curtains, tablecloths, etc., which are to be discarded.

"This not only keeps down WEEDS, but it serves to keep the ground from drying out.

SAVE YOUR HANDS

From Georgia: "I do a lot of gardening and yard work, but I seem to be all thumbs if I wear gloves, so my hands won't get stained.

"I have found that cuticle remover will REMOVE GRASS STAINS, sweet potato stains, and the stains in the little cuts I get when slicing vegetables without using a cutting board.

"Cuticle remover will also remove nicotine stains from your fingers."

This is absolutely so. And it's inexpensive, too.

And did you know that it would also remove grease stains from the crinkles on husband's or son's hands after they have worked on an automobile?

Pour some on, rub and massage the hand, and let remain a few minutes. Then wipe on tissue and wash as usual.

GARDEN GEMS

From Georgia: "Don't throw away your old wooden or metal venetian blinds; they make ideal decorator FENCES for your flower gardens.

"Long slats can be cut in half, then inserted in the ground; the small size need not be cut. Just depends on the height of fence you want.

"I also cut up plastic bottles and make permanent TAGS FOR MY PLANTS.

"I punch a hole in one end of each tag, slip some string through the hole and mark the tag with a waterproof pencil or ink brush.

"My garden problem of knowing what's planted where is solved."

When your rubber or nylon garden hose develops several leaks, don't throw it out . . . just make some more holes in it and you have a SPRINKLING HOSE for watering the lawn!

BE GOOD TO GARDEN TOOLS

To remove RUST FROM GARDEN TOOLS, dip a soap-filled steel wool pad in pure kerosene or turpentine and scrub away.

When most of the rust has been removed and while the fluid is still on the tool, wad up a piece of foil and rub it briskly. I am sure you will find most of the rust gone. Naturally, this will not fill up the holes if pitting has taken place. But it will prevent further rusting and help prolong the life of your tools.

Fancy Is Fun

We've all seen how clever, fancy touches make everyday things just a little bit nicer. I think that people who have the knack for these touches acquire it by asking themselves when things come up, "Now, what's the NICE way to do this?" (I DON'T mean the expensive way!) Once you get into this habit of thinking, how can anything be dull? Here's an example of what I mean.

I needed fresh PLACE MATS, so . . . I bought two yards of adhesive-backed paper for less than a dollar and made four place mats (18″ x 12″). Naturally, I did not remove the paper backing!

Place mats are very attractive when made with pinking shears, or they can be scalloped around the edges with regular scissors.

The mats are easy to keep clean, as they do not absorb

183

stains, and can be washed with a swipe of a damp sponge. They are much less expensive than the usual place mats.

You can cut the place mats any shape you like. I made a darling set by drawing around a turkey platter. And with the two-thirds of a yard I had left over, I could cut attractive centerpieces, or small circles to use as coasters for my glasses, water pitcher, etc.

I also covered my stained hot pads (the kind you set hot food on) with some of the scraps and they are prettier than they were when new. Now I have a matching set of EVERYTHING.

I think these would be wonderful to sell at bazaars and excellent as a project for Girl Scouts, etc. And think of the profit an organization could make with very little effort!

Here's another table-dress-up notion, this one for card players.

Whether you know it or not, expensive plastic playing cards should never be used on a card table unless it is covered. It ruins the cards—so say the manufacturers.

I made the cutest CARD TABLE COVER with a little over a yard of remnant of black velveteen (my furniture is ebony), and put a four-inch square of waterproof material on the top of each corner for coffee cups, etc.

The cards scoot across the lovely velveteen, which looks so expensive—but wasn't. I've had so many compliments on my cover, just thought I should pass the hint along.

A LITTLE IMAGINATION

From Pennsylvania: "I have a decorating idea for my DINING ROOM TABLE that I have found to be both practical and festive for holidays.

"Last year, I bought a clear plastic tablecloth to put over my regular cloth.

"Then I cut pictures from a magazine (Santa Claus, reindeers, etc.) and put them underneath the plastic at our individual places. I also cut out snowflakes in different colors and placed them here and there under the plastic tablecloth.

"The pictures can be changed with the season. On Valentine's Day, I put the valentines under the cloth and for Easter, I use pictures of bunnies and Easter eggs. The children love it."

BOWL 'EM OVER

From Illinois: "My husband prefers CARRYING LUNCH to work to eating at the coffee shop.

"Instead of a paper bag or a tin lunch box, we have found that a bowling shoe bag is the ideal way to carry a lunch.

"The bowling bag zips open easily, holds the smallest-to-the-tallest vacuum bottle, a spoon and even fruit and sandwiches. It also has a lovely carrying strap."

DRESS UP A TRUNK

Hint from a coed: "Trunks or FOOTLOCKERS are so handy for taking back to school, but they're often a nuisance for storing. I made a dust ruffle and a cushion (to match my curtains) for my footlocker. Now I have a seat for two people and don't have to worry about storing the trunk. The extra space in the trunk is also ideal for tucking away that extra ironing and for storing off-season clothes."

SLEEP TIGHT

This suggestion is written for those of you who have cold shoulders.

For years I had a quilted COMFORTER that just wouldn't stay up around my shoulders. Then the light-in-my-belfry finally turned on. I had planned to bind it with some corduroy left over from a bedspread I made. (Corduroy comes in different widths.) But I thought, "How much protection is a two-inch binding on my good comforter, anyhow?"

So, I nonchalantly covered the head of our comforter with the whole piece of corduroy . . . blankets may be done the same way.

This means that I basted some corduroy across the width of our comforter, putting half on the top of it and folding it back to the underneath side and basting it. This makes about twenty-two inches of protection for the comforter on each side.

Let me tell you what this does beside protecting the comforter or blanket: It lends weight. It HUGS your shoulders. The corduroy has a NAP and the nap is CROSSWISE (I put it straight across the top of the comforter). The nap KEEPS the blanket or comforter hugged on your cold shoulders. I am asking you to try it. Amazing what a help it is. So watch your sales in the paper and buy a few yards of corduroy on sale. Try it.

After all, you can remove the corduroy and use it for something else if you don't like it, but I would like to make you a little bet . . . you'll never take it off to use for something else. I never will.

Be sure to just TACK it onto the top and underside of your blanket or comforter and see what comfort (no pun intended) you get that you have never had before when trying to get a good night's sleep.

And isn't the first twenty-two inches of our blankets where the most soil accumulates? When necessary just untack the corduroy and wash only that.

THERE *IS* A PLACE FOR EVERYTHING

Once in a while something like this happens in our home that brings a good laugh.

I had two plastic STACK-STYLE VEGETABLE BINS standing by the front door (waiting to take them to the garage so my husband could use them for tools, etc.).

In came guests. It had been raining. They arrived with umbrellas, overshoes and wet mittens. One guest exclaimed, "Oh, Heloise, what a brain you are! How did you ever figure this out? And to think it has a place for my dripping wet umbrella, too. . . ."

I gasped. . . .

One guest immediately put her collapsible umbrella in the hollow tube which caught the drips, removed her overshoes and placed them in the bin part (where the potatoes usually go) and then put her son's wet boots in the bin.

What price discovery? Who knows? I never intended it for that purpose, but it was such a good idea that now we use it every time it rains.

P.S. These bins are also wonderful on front porches and back porches . . . the postman can use them for excess mail, the milkman can put your milk in them, etc.

From Pennsylvania: "My most frustrating problem has been what to do with various rolls of wrapping: waxed paper, foil, plastic wrap, etc.

"Recently I found that I could insert six rolls, in their cutter boxes, in a king-sized soft-drink carton by standing the boxes on end.

"This way they can be stored under the sink, in the pantry, or wherever you have room.

"This idea could also be useful with rolls of gift-wrapping paper."

COLD WEATHER WELCOME

From Maine: "When DOORKNOBS turn as cold as ice in the winter from snow and cold weather, I have a perfect solution: I gather up old earmuffs and pull off the fur parts that warm the ears. The fur pieces fit perfectly over the cold doorknobs!

"Since earmuffs come in a variety of colors they can match either the paint on the house or the color of the room, and make a pretty decoration. (They also prevent shocks when touching knobs.)

"All of my guests are delighted."

From Vermont, here's a hint for COZY FIRES: "Any time we eat oranges in our house I always make my family save the peelings.

"We accumulate them and toss them into the fireplace at home or into our campfire when we go on an outing. They are absolutely beautiful, give a nice aroma and pop and sparkle."

USE SOAP FRAGRANCES

From Tennessee: "When I come home from the grocery, I remove the wrappings from all bars of soap, and put some of them in my DRESSER DRAWERS. I have found that this not only helps prevent mildew, but it makes my clothes smell ever so lovely.

"This is especially good when used in linen closets, and the bars of soap are kept in among the pillowcases."

From Louisiana: "After airing my overnight bag or SUITCASE, I put a cake of unwrapped soap into it before putting it away.

"This eliminates that stale, musty odor."

KNITTING PRETTY

From North Carolina: "When winding YARN from a skein, if you encounter a knot in the yarn, place a different color yarn marker about a yard BEFORE the knot.

"This is a sort of signal that a knot is ahead, and knitting can be gauged to place knot at nearest seam edge or other inconspicuous place."

From Pennsylvania: "When winding YARN from a hank into a ball, I use a mothball as the core. This protects the yarn against moth damage when it is stored and not in use for some time."

NEAT TRICKS FOR THE KIDS

From Illinois: "I hung a three-pronged swing-away TOWEL RACK on the wall next to the dresser in my daughter's room.

"Each prong holds bracelets, necklaces, chains, etc., in apple-pie order. The rack is decorative, and best of all, no more tangled chains or lost charms."

From Georgia: "I have four little children, so it's always dirty hands and dirty towels. Just when I'm busy, one of the children needs a HAND TOWEL. It usually can be found on the floor in the bathroom or the kitchen. Well, I solved the problem: I went to the dime store and bought gripper snaps. I put three snaps at the end of each bath towel. When they are snapped over the bar, the rest of the towel hangs down so the small children can reach it. Now I

never find a towel on the floor, nor are they wadded up and thrown across the towel bar so they won't dry.

"Instead of grippers, big safety pins can be used. I used diaper pins with safety locks until I got around to buying the snaps."

HARDLY DISCARDABLE!

Here's the way I use PLASTIC SQUEEZE BOTTLES that contained liquid dishwashing soap: Starting approximately three inches from the bottom, I cut two-thirds of the way around the bottle, then cut upward and across to form a tab. This gives me a handy three-inch container with a tab for attaching it to a wall.

Heating an ice pick, I punch a hole in the tab so that it can be thumbtacked to wooden cabinets or hung from gummed picture hangers on metal surfaces. Then I decorate and label it with a felt-tip pen.

These containers are wonderful in the kitchen for matches, pins, stamps, coupons, soap pads, etc. Used on bathroom walls or cabinets, they hold razor blades, small medicine bottles, pill boxes, and other small items.

Place one at the proper height in your shower stall to hold shampoo . . . no more stooping or groping for the bottle of shampoo.

And, best of all, they never rust.

From New Hampshire: "If you should break the creamer of your good set of dishes, use the sugar bowl for a MAYONNAISE DISH. It will be real attractive and you will love it. The lid on the sugar bowl makes a good cover and keeps the mayonnaise from drying out."

From South Carolina: "When you empty your pencil sharpener, don't throw away the contents. Use the shavings to fill a small PINCUSHION for your sewing basket.

"The graphite in the shavings will keep your pins and needles sharp and rust-free. One of these makes a nice gift, too."

From West Virginia: "Did you know that an empty, clean, Worcestershire SAUCE BOTTLE makes a dandy vinegar dispenser for table use?

"With the label washed off, it is neat, compact, and so serviceable."

CREATIVE GIFT-GIVING

Here's an area where you can really use fresh ideas. The present that's given in routine fashion isn't much of a present at all, is it? So be thoughtful and original . . .

In each newly established household, there are innumerable tasks ahead: Curtain rods to hang, appliances to assemble, hooks to install, clothing poles to place, and many others.

As it usually falls to the husband, apprentice or veteran, to handle these "Honey-do" chores, I submit the following "Starter Kit":

A medium-weight claw hammer.
A pair of pliers.
A medium-size screwdriver.

A small versatile saw.
A good variety of screws, bolts, nails, brads and tacks.
A variety of accessory hardware—hooks, hanging aids, etc.

Naturally, this list could easily be expanded according to the experience and means of the giver, but, oh, how handy are just the above items for the new groom in the new household the first few weeks!

From Illinois: "To simplify and cut down the expense of GIFT-WRAPPING, I bought a roll of plain white shelf paper, and some of that tape that's sticky on both sides.

"For a baby shower, I just wrap the gift in the white paper and tape on some darling baby pictures cut out of a magazine.

"For a bridal shower I tape on a 'Heloise Bride'—a little clothespin face with pipe cleaner arms, and a bunch of little flowers in her hands. Her dress is a paper napkin folded from the corner, and the veil is a nylon net dishcloth.

"One can use any picture to fit the occasion. No ribbon is needed, and you will have different and attractive-looking packages."

From Wyoming: "When I discovered I was out of wrapping paper for a BRIDAL SHOWER, I wrapped my gift in a new (pretty) bath towel and tied it with ribbon. The bride-to-be was delighted."

LETTERS THEY'LL LOVE TO RECEIVE

From Kansas: "For special occasions, such as birthdays, get-well, etc., I always make my own GREETING CARDS to send to members of my family and special friends.

"They are cut from colored art paper. Pictures, flowers,

193

and little appropriate verses (which can be cut from any used card) or notes are included. Envelopes are made to match the cards.

"The homemade cards seem to be much more appreciated than the store-bought variety."

From Ohio: "I correspond frequently with a few friends.

"When answering a letter, I always make a CARBON COPY and staple the letter to a carbon copy of my answer.

"In this way, when I receive another letter from that same person, I do not repeat what I wrote in my last letter.

"This also serves as a diary of sorts."

From Maine: "I have found over the years that the very best way to write a long and interesting letter to loved ones away from home is to keep an envelope addressed to that person in my stationery box.

"As the days go along I put little things of interest in each envelope . . . a joke that was clipped from a magazine that might pertain to her or him, a snapshot, a recipe, a newspaper clipping, or just a cute drawing done especially for Grandma by the children.

"I also keep a pad of paper in the box so I can jot down notes from time to time about incidents I want to remember to include in the letters.

"When LETTER-WRITING TIME comes I am all ready to go, with never an excuse that there's no news or 'I don't know what to write about.' "

DON'T BE DOWN-CAST

Two years ago I had my arm in a CAST, and I can sympathize with all of you unfortunate skiers, tree climbers and others who have an arm or leg in a cast. It's awful.

A cast does get soiled, since one has to wear it a long

time. But you don't have to be content with it that way. It has been researched and found that white shoe polish may safely be applied to cover the soil. (I suggest that you dilute it with water, and apply with a piece of cotton.)

OR: When the cast is fresh and new, or later when it is soiled, just cut off the foot of a nylon stocking and pull the tube over the cast!

In addition to the stocking being flesh-colored and natural-looking, it will not only keep soil from accumulating on the cast itself, but your clothing slides over it beautifully.

I put TWO stockings over my cast to make it even more natural-looking.

On the same subject, a lady in Pennsylvania suggests another use for nylon net: "My husband had an accident, and his arm is in a CAST. There are professional slings which can be bought but they are not as nice in appearance as the nylon net sling I made for him. One yard will make two slings, providing a spare.

"As the net comes in seventy-two-inch width, I just cut it in half (making two squares), then fold it once into a triangle.

The net can be bought in colors to match the upper garment. (Example: Navy for dark suits. White for sport shirts, etc.)

"Once tied, it will not loosen from position. A musician's strap can be used for cushioning along the back of the neck if necessary."

FANCY YOU

From Rhode Island: "Many of us have earrings that we never wear because they hurt our ear lobes.

"Well, I have discovered a method that works wonders. "Cut off a tiny piece of moleskin corn plaster and stick it to the underneath flap of the earring! Now I can wear all my earrings without that nagging pain. (Moleskin can be puchased at a drugstore or dime store.)

From New Jersey: "If you have an IMITATION PEARL ring, earrings, etc., that is scratched or dull-looking, just give the pearls a coat of white nail polish, and they will look new and lovely.

"This polish is also wonderful as a glue, when replacing imitation pearls in pieces of jewelry.

"I use regular, colorless polish as glue in replacing other stones in jewelry, and it doesn't discolor the stones, as certain types of glue are apt to."

From New York: "When you tie HAIR RIBBON into a bow, have you ever wished the ends of the ribbon would stay even, without unraveling?

"Whether you cut the ribbon straight across or at an angle, try putting a little clear fingernail polish on the very ends of the ribbon. They will stay crisp for a long time."

I have found that stringing my beads on fishing line makes them much stronger, yet the line is fine enough to go through the smallest of beads. Try it, gals. You won't even need a needle.

TINTED SUGAR

"I love to give teas, coffees, or showers, but I seem to be in a rut. . . .

"Can you think of some little thing which is really different that I might do to add a little color and zest to the tea table?"

You really want something colorful? This might not knock 'em cold but it is a conversation piece:

How about making some pretty, pastel sugar?

Put half a cup of sugar in a cup or very small bowl and put three drops of food coloring in it. IMMEDIATELY, take a spoon and mix it, mix it, and remix it until the sugar is colored evenly.

Let it dry thoroughly (overnight at least), then mash it again.

Now, mix this dyed sugar with some *more* white sugar, adding white sugar gradually until you get the shade you want.

It's beautiful!

Why not make pale pink sugar for the coffee (especially pretty if you have a pink cake)?

I surely hope this helps you . . . it only costs about a zillionth of a cent, and where can you buy anything for that today?

Happy tinting.

TINTED RICE

With all the weddings taking place nowadays, we have been asked for something that might be different, inexpensive and fun.

Well, why not *tint* some rice to shower the bride and groom?

Or some of it wrapped in a piece of nylon net to match your color scheme, is also a darling favor at any bridal shower!

I suggest buying at least three boxes of REGULAR rice (*not pre-cooked*). If you don't use it all, you can always cook it and eat it later. Pour a half cup of cold water into a bowl and add a few drops or so of food coloring (until the desired shade is attained), then pour two cups of the *uncooked* rice into this mixture and immediately stir, stir, and stir with a spoon. (If the rice is too dark, add MORE rice at once and stir some more).

Now pour the rice on folded newspapers (this will absorb the moisture) and spread it with the spoon.

Every 30 minutes or so, stir the rice again—takes about three or four times—until it is *completely* dry. You can use your hair dryer. Or put it on a cookie sheet in a slow oven.

Make more than one shade and color in separate batches. Try pink, blue, yellow and a mixture of colors.

After these three or four mounds of rice are dry (each will be a different shade), mix them all together and add lots of white rice to those delicate little seeds of good wishes.

Oh, it's absolutely beautiful.

At my son's wedding, each guest was given a little bag of this rice upon entering the church. They all loved it.

The thought each guest enjoyed the most (I guess), is that each had individually participated when the bride and groom departed.

Recently, one friend packed a few tablespoons of this tinted rice in little pink net squares, tied them with pretty ribbon and stacked these around the centerpiece at a shower. Lovely.

Keepsakes are wonderful, aren't they?

And happy wedding to those of you who are embarking on the sea of matrimony. Keep those stars in your eyes . . . they are lovely.

All in the Family

"Occupation, Housewife" means doing countless little jobs every day, being all things to all people, and having all the answers.

The hints in this chapter dealing with children and family matters will make Occupation Housewife easier and fun, and save you all kinds of wear and tear.

WAYS WITH DIAPERS

From Illinois: "When my baby had DIAPER RASH, I found that disposable diapers were a wonderful help in curing it.

"Since these disposable diapers are lined on the outside with a wet-proof material, no rubber pants are necessary, and the air is allowed to circulate under the diaper, thus helping to cure the rash.

"The disposable diapers are just as absorbent as the regular diapers, and if used only for such emergencies and for traveling, are not too expensive." They also save mother much valuable laundering time.

From New York: "I keep a two-foot square of plastic in BABY'S DIAPER BAG.

"When visiting, and baby has to be changed, I lay the plastic on the couch or bed where baby is to have his diaper replaced.

"In this way, there is no danger of soiling my hostess' furniture covering."

BUNDLING BABY

From Utah: "Here is a hint that I think may help all mothers with SMALL BABIES.

"I found that my baby kept slipping to the side of his stroller even when he was reclining. Then a friend showed me this trick: I take a receiving blanket the baby has outgrown, fold it in half, roll it up and fasten it with three rubber bands.

"I make two of these blanket rolls and put one on each side of him whenever I take him out in the stroller, and whenever he needs bolstering in his high chair. This makes all his furniture fit him and prevents many bumps."

A MUST FOR EVERY CRIB

From South Dakota: "When my boys were very small I attached a metal towel rack to the end of each CRIB on the outside.

"This rack saved many steps. I used it to hold blankets, towels, etc. It's quite safe, especially if you attach it to the lower part of the baby's bed about at mattress level.

"Now that my boys are older, I have towel racks attached to the backs of their bedroom doors so that they can hang their trousers over them. Prevents wrinkles."

SLEEPY-TIME MENAGERIE

This delightful idea came from a mother in New Hampshire: "Instead of darning the holes in baby's KNITTED CRIB SHEETS (as I painstakingly did when I had only one imp—now there are three preschoolers), I make animals, designs, etc., with colored iron-on mending tape. The children love the patches, and your imagination is your only limit.

"One sheet has a small striped fish following a larger fish of the same design . . . a small hole was near a larger one!

"Another sheet has a smiling black whale spouting a white cloud of whatever whales spout!

"My children sit entranced watching me mend the sheets into animal playgrounds and oceansful of fish."

BABY'S SHOES

From Ohio: "Here's a wonderful method for cleaning and polishing BABY'S WHITE SHOES: First I clean the shoes with a rag and some rubbing alcohol, then polish as usual with white polish. (I have never had this hurt any of my baby's kid shoes.)

"When the shoes are completely dry, I take transparent boot polish (wax) and apply it to the shoes. When the wax is dry, I buff the shoes to a beautiful shine.

"The wax prevents the white shoe polish from rubbing off on mother's dark clothes!"

From Michigan: "If your small children have the LACE-TYPE SHOES, take four pretty matching buttons and attach them to the ends of the laces. The laces won't keep pulling through the holes and the buttons also add an attractive, decorative touch."

From Minnesota: "I got tired of clatter and scuffed baby shoes, so I carpeted my BABY'S STROLLER.

"Carpet samples are the perfect size.

"I took one of those gadgets you use to put metal eyelets in belts and punched holes in the front and back of the carpet, then just laced it to the stroller with a long shoelace.

"Easy to remove and wash. Keeps baby's feet warmer, saves on shoes and nerves."

From New York: "I tried tape and sanding the SOLES of my baby's shoes, but they were still slippery. Then I bought some very thin foam rubber (about one-eighth-inch thick) and glued it to the soles of his shoes. Results—no more falls.

"When this piece of foam rubber has worn off, take a razor blade and scrape off the remains and apply a new piece. Works beautifully."

'TWIXT BATH AND BED

From Rhode Island: "When our little kiddies are bathed and we put on their SLEEPERS (with feet in them), they always like to run around the house for an hour or so before they are tucked into bed.

"To prevent the soles of the feet from becoming soiled, I put a pair of daddy's dark stretch socks over their footsies!

"When tuck-in time comes, the socks are removed.

"Sure save pre-spotting sleepers on washday."

THE IN'S AND OUT'S OF IT

From California: "Here's a hint I hope you'll like for a boy who can't learn to keep his SHIRTTAILS tucked in.

"Just sew some lace on the hem of the shirt! That will teach him to keep it tucked in!"

LESS MESS AT FEEDING

From New Jersey, a wonderful way with toddlers: "When FEEDING my BABY, I put her in the playpen standing up—then I begin to feed her. She MUST hold on to the sides of the playpen with her hands.

"This keeps her from putting her hands in her mouth or hitting the spoon or reaching for more food!"

From Hawaii: "I have a suggestion for KEEPING BABY CLEAN while feeding him.

"I had the problem of food running out of his mouth, milk drooling down his neck, under the bib, and staining his collars, necklines, etc. So I now follow the procedure used by beauticians and barbers: I take a double thickness of facial tissue and tuck it in around his neckline under the bib.

"Now, when food gets under the bib, it is absorbed by the tissue, thus preventing stains and endless changing and washing of his clothing."

BABY BOTTLES

"For those who have little ones who are at the age of throwing their bottles out of the crib, here is a tip:

"Using my five-year-old's unmatched socks, I cut off the foot, seamed the leg part on one end and slid the bottle inside.

"These covers prevent dents or scratches on floors, eliminate some of the noise when the bottle hits the floor, save on bottles . . . and they look cute, too!"

BABY BOTTLE DEPOSITS

"After sterilizing baby bottles in hard water over a period of time they sometimes get that white, chalky deposit which is so hard to remove.

"If you will boil them in vinegar water (one cup of vinegar to a pot of water), put the bottles in and let them boil for 20 minutes or so you'll be surprised to see that the chalky substance wipes off with a clean towel."

Mommies, take note!

This works beautifully.

BOTTLE WARMERS

"I am surprised at the number of new mothers who complain of ruined pans from warming bottles and baby food.

"I have an excellent pan for this use . . . a metal coffee can! When lime deposits ruin it, I merely throw it away and start using a new one. Coffee cans are great for boiling eggs in, too."

If one doesn't have a coffee can, any large metal can, such as the kind fruit juice comes in, would do.

WEAN BABY

"When you think it's time to wean the baby and he just doesn't . . . remove the lid from the baby bottle and start him cup-drinking directly from his old favorite . . . his same bottle.

"Sure worked for me."

COOLING BABY BOTTLES

"Here's a hint for busy mothers with new babies and the problem of cooling too-hot bottles:

"After preparing the baby's formula, I place the excess formula into a previously sterilized jar and keep it in the refrigerator.

"If, while warming a bottle, it becomes too hot, I place a small amount of the cold formula in the bottle, thereby cooling the milk instantly.

"I also keep a jar of cold sterilized water to be used for the same purpose.

"This eliminates the tedious ordeal of holding the too-hot bottle under the water faucet to cool."

EASIER EATING FOR TOTS

From Pennsylvania: "I have triplets. I had such a hard time TEACHING THEM TO DRINK from a cup (it always spilled) that one day it dawned on me to wash their baby-food jars, fill them, screw the top back on, use a beer-can opener to punch a small hole in the top of the jar lid near the edge, and let the kids drink away all by themselves.

"The little jars are just the correct size for baby's tiny

hands, as they are already used to their bottle. The children certainly learned to drink in a hurry and it's only a skip to a regular glass after this."

From Ohio: "My little one loves HOT DOGS on a bun, but I find he can't open his mouth wide enough to get a bite.

"My solution to this problem is to take a ready-made refrigerator-type biscuit, flatten it out, and roll it around the hot dog. Then I put it in the oven for ten minutes, and I have a hot dog on a bun thin enough for a two-year-old's mouth.

"For real small tots, the frankfurter could be sliced in half lengthwise before rolling the biscuit around it."

From Colorado: "When preparing EGGS FOR MY CHILDREN, I first use an animal-shaped (or other odd-shaped) cookie cutter and cut out the center of each slice of bread after buttering it.

"I fry the egg in the empty space in the bread, turning the bread and egg over at the same time with a spatula to brown both sides of the bread.

"I also fry the cut-out parts. The children have the toasted animal to eat with the rest of the egg and bread.

"My children are now avid egg eaters!"

The eggs may either be fried whole or beaten as for scrambled eggs and poured into the center for cooking.

NUTRITIONAL TRICKS

Here are some ideas for getting the full nutritional value from the food you pay so much for at the market.

From New York: "I find it wasteful to discard the remains of jars of BABY FOOD after feeding my two-month-old her maximum of one tablespoon of the fruit or vegetable. Now, I divide the contents into individual plastic ice-cube containers, which I then put in the freezer.

"Every day I defrost one cube of the particular foods I want to feed her. This not only saves on the food, but it also allows for greater variety."

From Louisiana: "If I run short of regular milk and want to make up some NON-FAT DRY MILK, I open an empty, regular milk carton top as wide as possible, measure the amount of powdered milk wanted, pour it into the carton, and stir in the necessary amount of water.

"Then I staple the top back together, leaving the pouring spout open.

"This may be a bit sneaky, but my children drink the milk substitute sooner when it is served from the familiar carton rather than from the pitcher."

From Pennsylvania: "Here is one of my son's favorite HOT SCHOOL LUNCHES: I put two heated wieners in a wide-mouth vacuum bottle, then pour in hot soup.

"I put prepared hot dog buns in a sandwich bag, and put a fork in his lunch box to fish the wieners out of the soup, and a spoon to eat the soup with.

"Not only does he have a hot wiener on his bun, but the nice hot soup as well."

From New Jersey: "For those who have trouble getting their children to eat BREAKFAST: While visiting with my grandchildren, I noticed that they were expected to eat soon after they got out of bed, and they had very little appetite.

"So I suggested to my daughter that they all have a run up the road first—just for five minutes.

"They all came back to eat more and with less urging than before.

"Incidentally, I went with them the first time but since I'm on a diet, I'll stay home from now on!"

EASY SCHOOL LUNCHES

From Connecticut: "Making SANDWICHES is a real morning chore for mothers who have several children in school.

"Let the youngsters help you make the sandwiches during the weekend. They will love to choose their own fillings and will look forward to finding the sandwiches (which they made) in their lunches.

"I have found that some of the fillings which freeze best are leftover sliced roast beef, luncheon meats, baked ham, chicken, turkey, dried beef, sliced cheese or cheese spreads, hard-cooked egg yolks (the whites of hard-boiled eggs have a tendency to become tough when frozen) and peanut butter.

"Wrap the sandwiches separately, label them and put them in the freezer.

"The sandwiches can be put into the lunch pail without thawing, and by noon, they will be completely thawed."

BREAD SNATCHERS

From Quebec: "For those of you whose boys just will not close the end of the BREAD WRAPPER after taking out a piece of bread . . . keep a plastic bowl cover handy and show the boys how to place it over the open end of the loaf. They will then do this every time . . . I hope."

WIENEES FOR TEENIES

From Wyoming: "You can prevent children from getting scorched hands when ROASTING HOT DOGS if you poke their roasting sticks through those throw-away aluminum pie pans, which will serve as shields."

CHOOSE A BOOSTER

People probably have been trying to figure out answers to this one since the beginning of time. The telephone book is one way. Here are two other good ideas for boosting children up to the dinner table. And neither one costs much.

From New Hampshire: "My husband made BOOSTER SEATS for our children's regular use on our dining room chairs.

"He cut a piece of plywood the same size and shape as our chair seats, attached four blocks of wood about three or four inches high.

"He padded the top of the board with a piece of foam, then we covered these booster seats with the same material with which we had covered our chairs.

"When not in use, the boosters are hardly noticeable.

"When you must use a book or two to boost a young child to the table, put a plastic place mat over them (preferably one with a backing so the child won't slip).

"Any accidental spills or the inevitable crumbs won't mar the books."

A family in Indiana did it this way: "We needed a chair to boost our two-year-old up to the table but had no room for another high-chair or stool.

"My husband took a plastic wastebasket of medium size (one that stands flush with the floor) and put a toss pillow snugly into the bottom of it. Then with tin snips he cut away part of the front and sides, making a very attractive 'bucket seat.'

"Be sure the pillow is a tight fit. It can be covered with plastic for easy cleaning.

"This bucket seat sits on a regular kitchen chair, and we also use it in the car, fastening the seat belt around it and the child, so that she can see out the window while sitting as we are riding.

"The children also use it on the floor as a toy chair for dolls.

"The total cost was under two dollars."

PARTY NOTIONS

The expenses of giving a children's party can really add up, so save your pennies where you may. Here are some ideas that will look extravagant, but actually cost you very little.

From New York: "Here's a cute way to make PARTY INVITATIONS for children:

"Blow up balloons and write the invitation on them with a felt marker or crayon.

"Let the balloons dry, deflate; then mail them to the children in envelopes.

"I have used this balloon idea for several years and it is always a hit with the children, as they blow up the balloon to see what's written on it and find an invitation to a party."

From Ohio: "I am fourteen years old and here's a different TRICK FOR A CHILDREN'S PARTY: Place a marshmallow in each section of your ice tray, add water and freeze the cubes. They really pep up a soft drink and are so attractive.

"Besides, when the cubes partially melt, the marshmallows can be eaten."

From South Dakota: "For children's birthday parties, I put a double thickness of cupcake liners in my muffin tins, fill each one with ICE CREAM, and store them in my freezer until serving time.

"One can also decorate the tops with candies or even candles. This prevents last-minute rush and melted ice cream."

HAIRCUT REHEARSAL

From Georgia: "When my husband and I took our oldest son for his FIRST HAIRCUT, it was all we could do to hold him still. He screamed and cried because he was so frightened.

"After that ordeal I invented a little game. I put the child in his high chair, pinned a towel around his neck, and got out the scissors, comb and brush.

"I then pretended to cut his hair. I used the brush as the clippers and buzzed around his ears, making a noise like the clippers. The next time he had his hair cut there wasn't a whimper.

"This idea also worked with our second little boy, and here's hoping it will work for the third!"

From California: "Here is a good way to prepare a little one for his FIRST HAIRCUT:

"While you are using your electric razor, let the side of it slide on his neck.

"He will get used to the sound of it after a few times, and won't be frightened when it comes time for the haircut.

"I did this, and it worked fine."

TRY A WEEKLY KIDS' DAY

From Connecticut: "I'm a busy mother of several small children. Two of my neighbors and I have a marvelous co-operative scheme.

"We each have 'KIDS' DAY' one day a week. On that

day nothing else is planned. We have nursery school at our house for our own and two other neighbors' pre-schoolers.

"In this way, our little ones receive guidance at the beginning of their social development, learn to be away from mommy, and to play with other youngsters.

"Too, they have the benefit and variety of a sizeable number of toys to enjoy.

"On the moms' side: When there's nothing else on the agenda, it's a lot of fun. No fights! No cross moms!

"Then, there are those FREE days each week.

"Our wee ones are very happy children, who aren't in trouble in our neighbors' yards when out playing, or running into danger's way.

"And, mommy misses them when they are away, and welcomes them home with open arms, and they say hello with a big hug. It is really wonderful."

HELP THEM LEARN

From New York: "A hint to mothers of babies LEARNING TO CRAWL: If the baby scoots on his tummy and can't get the technique, try crawling around the floor with him

"I taught my two youngsters to crawl this way in hardly any time at all."

From Vermont: "I would like to tell parents who help their first-grade children with ARITHMETIC, addition and subtraction problems about a wonderful method I have found: Take a calendar and cut out the numbers on the calendar in squares. Since a calendar has twelve months of numbers, this provides a large number of figures to work with.

"Lay these numbers out on the kitchen table and play with them as you do anagrams.

"The child can pick any two numbers, such as 1 and 3. Then the mother asks him to add or subtract them.

"This is fun for the child, especially if the mother will allow the child to cut the calendar up himself. I suggest that a mother get a calendar with large numbers. They are easier for the child to see and it is more enthralling for him.

"Once the child has figured out all of the problems that have been laid out, just mix the numbers up and let the child add or subtract them again."

From California: "For those assorted INSECTS, BUGS, ETC., that all children find and want to keep for a little while. . . .

"Any jar can be topped with a piece of nylon stocking held in place by a rubber band. This will allow plenty of air, and a little water can be dropped through the nylon.

LITTLE ARTISTS

From Connecticut: "Have you ever thought about letting little tots use FINGER PAINTS in the bathtub?

"After having finger paints spread all over my porch, the breakfast room table and the kids' bedrooms, it hit me like a ton of bricks!

"Now, I take off all the children's clothes (I happen to

have two) except their pants and put them in the empty bathtub. They can spread their paper on the smooth surface on the inside of the tub. They can put their paints on the edge of the bathtub and make all the mess they please.

"At least, this is the most terrific answer to save my *nerves* that I have ever found. Why? Because, all I have to do is collect the papers, pick up the paints and put them in a cardboard box, remove the kids' undergarments, fill the bathtub with suds and away they go!

"They love it; so do I. Of course, I always keep a close eye on them, and they know not to turn on the water faucets. The most important point of this is that while soaking in their nice soapy bath all the paint comes off of them too!"

From New York: "I have discovered a way to keep children's MODELING CLAY soft and pliable. Enclose it in a tight jar with a small piece of damp cloth. Hard clay can also be softened the same way."

TOYS TO MAKE

It is possible to keep small children endlessly amused with toys made from available household items. They're even fun for mother to make, and while she is doing it she can smile at the fact that it's not costing her a cent.

From California: "For those with small children who like simple JIGSAW PUZZLES, here is a very inexpensive way to make one.

"Take a picture from a magazine and paste it on a thin piece of cardboard. Trim the cardboard to fit the picture. One could also use a picture from a child's worn-out storybook.

"Cut it into odd pieces and shapes with a scissors. Put the pieces in a box and label it.

"You will have as good a puzzle as any bought in a store."

From Vermont: "If mothers with small children will save the plastic containers which tomatoes are sold in, they will find that the children love PLAYING TRAIN with them. These little plastic containers can be tied together with string and loaded with freight.

"After the children tire of this, they can build other things with the containers simply by tying them together differently."

From Washington: "Here's a hint for rainy days for children.

"If you save PLASTIC LIDS from coffee cans (and I hope you do), give the children some, along with a pair of scissors, tape, string, ribbon, or shoelaces, and their crayons.

"Watch the lovely things they make with their own marvelous imagination. For example, my five-year-old made a set of colored flowers, made a hole in the center of each flower, then put a shoelace through them all. She held each end of the lace and had a 'whirlygig.'

"There's no end to the things that kids will make from these materials."

From New York: "I am a kindergarten teacher and we are going to make DRUMS out of coffee cans as a project. Here's how: Cut off the top and bottom of the can with a can opener—(being certain the edge is absolutely smooth) and put plastic lids (which come on the coffee cans) on both top and bottom. Glue construction paper around the sides of the can and decorate. Insert a piece of string with a knot on each end under each lid for a handle.

"These drums cost nothing and the children really love them."

From New Hampshire: "We saved up a set of plastic coffee-can covers, painted them black and red, and use them as a large-size CHECKER SET for our basement playroom floor."

LITTLE HELPERS

"I have an idea that is fine for mothers who have children old enough to push a grocery cart and check prices at the market.

"Write items that would be found in one area on a sheet of paper and give the list to one child. Write items found in another area on a separate sheet and give it to another child, etc. Let each child have his own cart.

"When the children have finished their SHOPPING tell them to meet in one place and put all the groceries into one cart.

"This saves time, is much more fun for the kids, and it teaches them how to shop."

From North Carolina: "I help my mother by taking the GARBAGE CANS out to the street for collection.

"The way I do this is to put the garbage can on a skateboard and roll it out!"

From Hawaii: "For perfect QUICKIE APRONS for your toddlers when they want to help with the dishes . . . just fold a bath towel in half over a string or ribbon and tie it way up under their arms.

"Gives over-all double protection!"

A modern Tom Sawyer who lives in Florida came up with this one: "My younger brother and I earn our allowances by performing duties around the house. One of our duties is to keep our rooms straightened. This includes dusting the furniture and cleaning the windows.

"My little brother refused to WASH THE WINDOWS until

I put the cleaning solution into one of his squirt guns. Now he cleans the windows in record time.

"He even uses a water-filled gun to help Mom dampen the clothes."

GIFTS TO THE KIDS

From Pennsylvania: "We have a flock of grandchildren and most of them are dating and using the family car.

"Dating seemed to be quite an expense for Mom and Pop when it came to buying gasoline for the auto, and this became a bone of contention in the family.

"When holidays rolled around, the PRESENTS FOR THE GRANDCHILDREN made quite a dip into our savings, as I could never find much they might appreciate for three dollars apiece.

"Now Granddad and I go to our favorite filling station and pay for 10 gallons of gas for each child who is old enough to drive. This leaves a credit for each one, and the gasoline can be used five gallons at a time, or anyway they see fit.

"For the grandchildren who live out of town, we just enclose three new one-dollar bills with a holiday card and say 'This is for gasoline for your next date.'

"Now, all the grandkids look forward to their gifts each year."

From Utah: "Only seven years ago all of our children were home.

"Now all the children are married into families with brothers, sisters, aunts and uncles and are raising families of their own. We were finding it a drain on our budgets when it comes to buying HOLIDAY or BIRTHDAY PRESENTS.

"I hesitated to bring this up, but last year I suggested

220

that we grownups all put our names in a pot, draw names from it, and limit each gift to five dollars. This wasn't supposed to include the tiny tots or the grandchildren, but the most amazing fact was that ALL the older children agreed to it too.

"I can just about guarantee that any mother or grandmother who mentions this idea to her family will find that the idea is most welcome.

"Not only does it save on budgets, but think of all the time it takes to TRY to find something that each individual needs or likes. Oh, dear me!"

From Vermont: "To make an attractive GIFT FOR SMALL CHILDREN, mount glow-in-the-dark decals on any chosen background and frame them.

"The designs are washable, sunfast and luminous. They are decorative during the day and help chase fears of darkness at night."

SHOW OF HANDS

Mothers of small children will be interested in this SAFETY PRECAUTION: A friend of mine has three little ones. When they get into the car, she lets the children get in first, then she says, 'Hands up! I am shutting the door.' When she sees all the little hands in the air she closes the door. No chance of smashed fingers this way."

SAVING A LIFE

Stop, look and READ! How would you like to help save someone's life?

Or prevent a serious injury to a little child or a visitor in your home?

So many times little children (especially the very young

ones) cannot read, or do not heed cautions on containers.

Many times, too, mothers and fathers do not read directions and cautions on bottles and containers. Some bottles do not even have the words "poison," "caustic," "toxic," etc., written on them even though their contents can kill or cripple a person.

So here is what I figured out for you mothers and fathers who have little children. It is also a good safety precaution for yourselves.

Do not delay. Go buy some dark red fingernail polish at your dime store. The brand or quality makes no difference in this case.

Take the little brush out of that bottle of dark red fingernail polish and completely PAINT every bottle cap and lid on such things as bleaches, ammonia, turpentine, kerosene, alcohol, disinfectants, insect sprays, spot removers, cleaners, etc. Include everything that would harm a child if swallowed.

Also paint a big "X" with that dark red fingernail polish on both sides of all these bottles and containers.

TEACH your child now that anything he sees with a red mark—either an "X" or a red cap or lid on it—means "No! NO! DANGER OR POISON."

Now is the time to teach your child what poison means and what your marks with the color red mean. Later, when he learns to talk and understand, you can explain it to him further.

He will use and reuse this red signal all his life. Even before he starts to school, he will learn that a red light means "stop," or "danger." (Later, when he drives a car and sees the red stop lights of a car in front of him go on, he will know it means stop, danger, etc.)

And let me give another little hint to all young mothers

who have small babies. Now is the time to take that bottle of fingernail polish and paint the hot water faucet in your bathtub, in your basin, and in your kitchen sink!

With your teaching, the little child will quickly learn that a red water faucet means danger. Don't forget, a little child sometimes doesn't know his left hand from his right hand, or a left faucet from a right one for many months. At least the poor little tyke will know that hot water is coming out instead of that cold water he expects when he goes to wash his hands. This will prevent many small scalded hands.

Do not worry about putting fingernail polish on your metal water faucets. It won't hurt them one bit. As soon as the child is old enough to clearly remember which is hot water and dangerous, all you have to do is take some fingernail polish remover and remove the red polish with some facial tissue. It comes off clean as a whistle, no matter how long it's been on the faucets.

If you think you are wasting your time by painting the tops of all those containers red, this is not so. Because the next time you buy a new bottle of bleach, ammonia, disinfectant, etc., all you have to do is remove that pretty, red "caution" top from the empty one and screw it on the new bottle . . .

Let's save a life and prevent injury any way we can.

Don't you be responsible for anyone's accident.

I love you all.

PLEASURES FOR PATIENTS

From Texas: "A muffin pan makes a darling BED TRAY for a sick child.

"Whether it has six or twelve cups makes no difference. Fill the ones nearest the child first. One will hold his small glass of milk, another his gelatin salad. The rest hold his crackers, the salt, pepper, mashed potatoes, green beans, etc.

"My kids simply love this trick."

From Washington, a thoughtful mother suggests: "When a member of the family is confined to bed, place a damp paper towel or damp paper napkin under the dishes on the BED TRAY!

"The dampness of the towel will prevent the dishes from slipping and can be used to clean the patient's fingers after the meal is finished."

From Maine: "If you have a small child sick in bed and do not have a BED TRAY for him, just take a heavy cardboard box and cut it down to the right height, then cut out a section on both sides so that the box will fit over his legs.

"It makes a perfect table for his tray or to use as a desk while he is ill."

Save on adhesive bandages—and tears—with this idea from California: "When a child gets a scraped knee or elbow, it is difficult to keep the BANDAGE in place.

"I cut the toe off an old clean white stretch sock, then pull the sock over the child's elbow or knee until the heel of the sock is over the kneecap or crazy bone, whichever the case may be.

"The stretchy sock will give with the child's movements but will hold the bandage in place and keep it from becoming soiled so rapidly."

A SOUND IDEA

"Here's a thoughtful present to give grandparents for Christmas—especially those who are far away:

"Last year, my wife and I sent a small TAPE RECORDER (less than $25.00 each), and bought one for ourselves, too.

"As all of us are lazy letter writers, this has been a blessing as we get to hear Mom's and Pop's voice not once, but many times. They in turn get to hear the children's voices. This they love.

"The tiny spools of tape cost about 35 cents but can be used over and over again.

"The greatest part about this is that we have it connected all the time, and when we think of something, we just pick up the mike and add to the tape."

IRRESISTIBLE TRANSISTORS

From Kansas: "I have a five-month-old son, and one day I was busy and could not entertain him. So I put him in his crib and turned on a small TRANSISTOR RADIO nearby. I tuned in to soft music. (If you search the dial, you can find nice music!)

"He was absolutely enchanted, and kept 'talking' to the radio. And mother could get on with her work!"

"PLAY ME THE THREE BEARS, MOMMY"

"I got so tired of telling 'The Three Bears' and the usual BEDTIME STORIES to our three little children that we finally put all their stories, in our own words, on the tape recorder!

"Now, just before bedtime each night, we turn on the tape recorder. They hear our voices and are completely enthralled with the story coming out of the tape recorder. Daddy tells one story and Mother tells the next.

"Last week we let each child tell her favorite story in her own words and put this on tape. You would be surprised how they love to hear that played back just before bedtime!

"This is a wonderful idea for those who do not have the energy to tell the same story over and over again, and just wait until you see the children's faces when they hear their own voices. It's worth its weight in gold."

MAIL HATH CHARMS

I've often thought how much more thoughtful we would be if only we had more time!

With this in mind, and knowing how little folks love to receive PACKAGES in the mail, I set a few hours aside occasionally to gather up and wrap little boxes for mailing to nieces, nephews and little friends. This way it takes only an hour or so to wrap enough packages for several months.

Don't wait for just birthdays or Christmas—send them often. What seems like junk to us, is fascination to small fry.

Keep an eye open for cute five-and-dime party favors. What look like special favors to us, are darling little umbrellas to them.

Put a little tag under the string or ribbon on each package which you have wrapped for mailing, so you'll know exactly what each box contains, and remove it before mailing.

From Michigan: "Two of my sons just left for the service. I write them letters often to help prevent 'away-from-home-blues.'

"They had the same friends and general interests, so in order to avoid having the second letter sound hastily written, I type a carbon copy of the first page, giving all the news about home to both boys.

"The second page I type 'for Nicky only' at the top, and proceed with personal remarks to him, then type a 'for Charles only' page.

"This way, I don't get tired and leave out anything, and

227

I don't put off writing. Also my attention is dispensed equally to each boy.

"This might help other mothers with 'boys in service.' "

HURRAY FOR US

Whoever has this Pennsylvania family rooting for their side is lucky.

"We cut plastic bleach bottles in half, and use the tops as MEGAPHONES to root for our team!

"We spray the megaphones with purple and gold (since those are our school colors) and they look like the real thing!"

BEST DRESSED DOLLS

From Utah: "A man's old tie, cut in sections, can be used to make CLOTHES FOR LITTLE GIRLS' LITTLE DOLLS. And those doll clothes can be expensive.

"By cutting the triangle off the end of Dad's old tie, then cutting a portion above that for the body of the dress, one has a darling sheath evening dress. This may either be cut with pinking shears or hemmed.

"The back portion of the tie can be used to make another dress.

"These dresses may be trimmed with sequins, lace, rhinestones, etc.

"Odd socks which are not too worn or faded may be cut

into three sections. The toe can be used for a hat, the mid or heel section for a purse, and the top for a knitted sheath dress. Either stretch sox or ribbed type can be used."

WAXED PAPER CAPER

If your children's BACK-YARD SLIDE has become rusty and is no longer slippery: Give each of the children a big piece of waxed paper and let them sit on it and go down the slide.

The more times they slide and the more waxed paper that is used, the slicker the slide becomes!

WALKER ON THE WALLS

"Our BABY'S WALKER was making horrible marks on the walls, and scratches on the furniture and doorways.

"My husband cut an old garden hose into strips, split them lengthwise through one side, and clamped them onto the metal bars on the walker that were causing all the trouble.

"The rubber not only protects the furniture from scratches, but if baby bumps into something, it acts as a shock absorber so he doesn't feel the bump so much."

RUBBERS IN A BASKET

From New Jersey: "When the snow and rain season is in full bloom, the front door seemed an endless mess of BOOTS AND RUBBERS until I solved the problem by putting a plastic clothes basket, lined with a plastic bag, by the front door. Now my rugs stay cleaner and there's no rushing around searching for boots and rubbers before school time.

"I also use the same kind of baskets for my youngest son's toys."

PRESCRIPTION: PRIVACY

If you have two children who are always quarreling because they SHARE A BEDROOM, try building a bookcase, or anything of the sort, three-fourths of the way to the ceiling and two-thirds the length of the room, and using it as a room divider.

This will give the children a sense of privacy.

FEEDING FIDO

From Georgia: "If you really want a happy, healthy dog, save all VEGETABLE WATERS (including potato), and mix them (instead of tap water) with your pet's dry dog food.

"Our little beagle likes it so much, he will even drink it plain, instead of water. Last night he enjoyed a 'green bean cocktail!' "

"The vet, whom we don't see very often, tells us he is the picture of health, so maybe it's because I don't throw vitamins down the drain."

From Florida: "I buy five- and ten-pound economy sacks of DRY DOG FOOD. I empty the dog food into one-pound coffee cans (with the plastic lids).

"Keeps from drawing bugs into the house, and it's easy to pour what you need out of a can."

From Kentucky: "My mother made the cutest 'dining room' for our dog! His WATER DISH AND FOOD DISH were always being upset or pushed around.

"She got a heavy cardboard box, removed the top and cut out all of one side of the box except for about an inch along the bottom (so the dishes wouldn't slide out), then she covered it inside and out with adhesive-backed plastic paper.

"It looks nice in the dog's special corner of the kitchen and saves us from having to mop up after an upset."

From Illinois: "When our dog has to take PILLS, I bury one at a time in a small amount of his canned dog food. No fuss and no taxed nerves."

PET PATTER

I remember helping a friend of mine round up puppies from all over an old-fashioned basement. If only she had corralled them the way this lady in Ohio does!

"An outgrown PLAYPEN is great when a new addition to the family—a puppy—comes along.

"Line the playpen with plastic and lots of newspapers, and there will still be room for a sleeping box.

"If the puppy is small enough to wiggle through the bars, line the sides with cardboard or chicken wire."

From Maine: "I do not put a COLLAR ON MY CAT, since he might catch it on something and strangle.

"Instead, I take a one-half-inch-wide piece of elastic and machine-stitch the ends together to make a collar that

231

will fit loosely around his neck. Then with an indelible pen, I write my telephone number and address on his collar.

"If the cat catches the elastic collar on something, he will be able to wriggle free. It may not be as pretty as a regular collar, but it is safer, washable, and easily replaced; and if you want a fancier one, you can always use decorative elastic."

PRETTIFIED POOCH

From New York: "We have an adorable little dog. He loves to take a BATH and then have his coat dried with my electric hair dryer.

"After bathing him, we put him inside a cotton pillow-case cover and zip up the zipper so that just his head is sticking out.

"Turn the hair dryer on medium-warm and insert the hose into the cotton case. It will blow up like a balloon.

"You can gently massage his fur through the heavy cotton while the warm air is going into the bag, and the doggie loves it.

"Be sure not to zip the zipper too tight. The air MUST escape somewhere.

"This is much quicker and more efficient than towel-drying."

From New Jersey: "For those who have a dog to bathe, make a 5" x 12" NYLON NET BAG. Cut a bar of dog soap into eight or ten pieces, put the soap in the bag, tie a big knot in the end of the bag and use it to scrub the dog.

"It's wonderful . . . one hand is free to hold the dog, no sponge needed and no lost soap. Cuts bath time in half!"

FOR THE BIRDS

I put a piece of ice (usually one cube) in the watering dish in my bird's cage. Much easier than carrying water. When the ice melts, the bird has COOL, FRESH WATER. Besides, my bird loves to play with the ice.

BIRDBATHS

"I have a hint for bird lovers who have birdbaths.

"To clean off the green fungus that grows in the bottom and on the sides of the bath, pour out any excess water, then wet paper towels and stick them to the sides and bottom of the bath.

"Pour some household bleach on the paper and let stand for 15 or 20 minutes. Remove the paper and wash the bath.

"This treatment sometimes kills the fungus for as long as six weeks."

We used to clean ours by filling it with clean water, pouring in one-half cup of bleach, scrubbing with a brush, letting stand awhile, then pouring out the water. (Be sure to cover with newspapers so a bird won't try to drink.)

Let this air for a few hours so the bleach will evaporate before refilling.

We also cleaned our small fish pond the same way. Removed all the algae and stains.

LINE BIRDBATH

"If you have a birdbath, you know how soiled and slimy the bottom can get.

"If you are tired of scrubbing it week after week, maybe this little tip will help you:

"After scrubbing the birdbath (for the last time) line it with plastic wrap off that roll in your kitchen!

"When you are ready to change the water next time, simply pour it out, replace the plastic and have a cleaner, more beautiful birdbath."

Helo-Easys

These savers are for those times when you're grumbling to yourself, "There must be an easier way to do this!" There usually is. The trick is in knowing how.

KITCHEN-EASYS

Who likes cleaning out those MESSY DRIP TRAYS below the burners on your stove?

Nobody! Next time they get filled with spilled-over food and grease clean 'em real good and then wrap the whole tray in foil. Take your sponge (if you use your hand, you might break the foil) and press the foil down to fit the tray perfectly, and slide it back in.

Result?

NEXT time, you will save about ten minutes cleaning those trays. All you have to do is change the foil.

From California: "Here is a time-saver I have used for years: I rub a thin coating of vegetable shortening on the threads and underneath the LIDS OF JARS used for storing liquids such as molasses, glue, touch-up enamel paints and so forth.

"Merely grease the threads of the caps. The lids will never stick tight.

"This is also wonderful for nail polish bottles, screws and bolts in stoves, and all appliances before they become frozen with age."

From New York: "After long use, VACUUM BOTTLE CORKS seem to shrink so that they are no longer tight enough for the bottle. Just boil the cork in a covered pan for a few minutes, and it will expand so that it will fit the bottle again."

Beats buying new corks for old bottles.

From Kentucky: "Here's a kitchen sight-saver: When the figures on your KITCHEN STOVE CONTROL become dim, take a black crayon and just color the whole kaboodle, Rub off the surplus with a soft cloth, and the figures will be just like new again."

From Louisiana: "Cut a piece of plastic wrap about ten inches square and put it on the refrigerator door where little hands (and big ones, too) are prone to leave FINGER MARKS.

"The plastic wrap sticks to the door, is hardly noticeable, and saves the door from constant cleaning.

"This could be used on any door where fingers may leave a mark. All you do is wipe the plastic wrap with a sponge. The marks come off beautifully."

THAT VERSATILE VACUUM CLEANER

From Illinois: "Here's a tip for inflating children's PLASTIC SWIMMING POOLS.

"Some tank-type vacuum cleaners have an opening for exhaust as well as the usual opening for sucking in dust. Just attach the sweeper hose to the exhaust side of your tank! Place the other end of the sweeper hose over the piece provided on the plastic pool for inflating. Turn on the sweeper and the air exhaust from the sweeper tank will inflate the pool in a few minutes with a minimum of effort."

This may not work on all pools but it does if the pool has the wide, fold-type opening. The plastic may be held against the nozzle of the vacuum. And don't forget when you deflate your pool the same vacuum can be used with a reverse method to remove all the air. Then the pool can be folded nicely.

From Maine: "This is a good hint for wives who have tried to DRY OUT HUNTING BOOTS overnight. I used to hang them upside down over a furnace, stuff them with paper and the like, but they were still almost impossible for my hunter to pull on for the next hunt. Then I found that if I reversed the vacuum hose on my vacuum cleaner (so it would blow), inserted it in the boot and let it run, the boots would be bone dry within minutes. Much comfort for him and what a time-saver for me!"

How about THAT? It also works on wet shoes. NEVER try

to dry boots over heat of ANY kind. RUINS leather! I know. I tried. They curled up and died.

From New Jersey: "Last summer we had DANDELIONS BLOOMING in our front yard. If I cut them, the fuzz (seeds) blew all over the yard.

"I took my vacuum cleaner outside and sucked up all the fuzz! The neighbors almost called the 'men-in-the-white-coats' to come get me!"

From New Hampshire: "I used the suction hose of my vacuum cleaner to CLEAN DUST MOPS, dust cloths and my carpet sweeper.

"It's wonderful and so easy to do in no time at all."

Gals, this idea is especially good for those of us who live in apartments. Managements do frown on shaking dust mops out of apartment windows!

From South Dakota: "I use the dusting brush on my vacuum cleaner for CLEANING SUEDE SHOES.

"It raises the nap and removes deeply imbedded dust."

BARBECUE-EASYS

From New York: "We live in an apartment building. There is no place for outdoor cooking, so we don't own a charcoal grill.

"However, we've found a wonderful substitute.

"When we go on a picnic, I take along an old oven

rack and we support the four corners of it with cans (large juice cans are best), then light the charcoal fire under it.

"It's wonderful for charcoaling steaks or hot dogs, or we can set our skillet on it for frying potatoes.

"The rack takes up no space when stored, and it can be kept in the trunk of your automobile.

"Why buy a new one when you can eat just as well off this HOMEMADE GRILL!"

For those of us who cook outdoors, here's the perfect way to clean that MESSY BARBECUE GRILL.

As soon as the grill cools, just lay it on the grass and leave it overnight. The dew works like magic. Amazing how easy it will be to wash the next morning."

BED TIPS

From Indiana: "I never knew where to put the bedspread when I took it off the bed at night. Then it occurred to me to put a TOWEL RACK on the back of the bedroom door. I now hang my folded bedspread on this rack.

"It seemed like such a good idea that I put up a second rack, about two feet higher, on the same door. On this one I hang a folded, extra blanket for cold nights. No more stumbling around or groping in the linen closet when I'm half asleep!

"There's only one thing wrong with this idea. My husband thinks the towel rack is a convenient place to hang his trousers and tie!"

What's the easiest way to make beds?

Never, ever walk around a bed more than is necessary to straighten sheets, blankets, spreads, etc.

Completely make one side of the bed, straightening all

the coverlets first, and then walk around to the other side and smooth out all the remaining wrinkles.

If necessary (if you have a king-sized bed), you can walk back around to the side you made first and straighten out the coverlets *once* more.

After you do this a week or so, you will see how much energy you are saving, and won't do it any other way. Why do you think hospital nurses use this method? (I was a Red Cross nurse's aide during World War II, and learned it then.)

PILLOW TALK

From Massachusetts: "I wonder if you know that you can put your FEATHER BED PILLOWS in a tumble dryer, and the pillows will fluff up like magic!

"I usually do this without heat. For those who have a heat-only dryer use on low heat. It will do as good a job.

"And the pillows smell nice and clean, too."

And those who sleep on any type of feather pillow should also "punch" the pillow from both sides and both ends each time they make their beds. This will also help keep them fluffy.

Here's a suggestion for when you are PUTTING NEW COVERS ON FEATHER PILLOWS: Insert two newspapers inside the new cover. Open one end of the old pillowcase, and gently insert it between the two newspapers.

Remove the pillow, shaking slightly to make the feathers ease down into the new cover. The feathers will slide on the paper, instead of sticking to the material. Remove newspapers and stitch open end of new case.

Less chance of flying feathers!

EASY WAYS . . . FOR PARTY-GIVERS

From Arizona: "When a crowd gathers for a party on your patio or in your yard, give them freewheeling service from your garden wheelbarrow!

"Scrub the barrow, line it with aluminum foil and fill it with ice.

"It's an IDEAL CART for bottled drinks, watermelons and great for keeping salads crisp and cold."

. . . FOR HARVESTERS

A FRUIT-PICKING POLE is an inexpensive tool for picking any kind of ripened fruit which grows a little too high to reach—and without having to use a ladder or climb the tree itself.

To make one just take any old cane fishing pole about twelve feet long and cut off the last few inches of the small end. This leaves a deep, open hollow in the small end of the pole.

Fasten a bag or sack to the end of the pole (a small gunny sack, orange sack, etc., will do). Straighten out an old wire clothes hanger. Bend this into a circle to fit around the top of the sack . . . then feed the wire in and around the top of the edge of the sack. Bend the other part of the wire coat hanger straight down and stick it into the open hollow end of the pole. That's all there is to it!

To pick the fruit simply raise the pole and ease the bag gently under the out-of-reach fruit. Wiggle the wire rim of the bag back and forth against the stem of the fruit. If the fruit is ripe it will fall easily into the bag.

Sure saves broken legs and arms—and lots of good fruit that might otherwise have gone to waste.

FOR DORMITORY DWELLERS

From Massachusetts: "I am a college student, and have a suggestion for a PORTABLE CARRY-ALL for anyone who lives in a dormitory.

"Get a plastic bucket—like the kind children use in a sandbox.

"It's great for carrying all the things you need from your room to the bathroom. It is almost impossible to carry soap, towel, washcloth, toothpaste, etc., without dropping something—so the bucket solves the problem.

"Nearly everyone at our college has one."

. . . FOR SHOE POLISHERS

"Now don't laugh, but I asked my wife to buy me a powder puff.

"No, I haven't flipped. I keep it in my can of wax shoe polish so it won't dry out. It's perfect for APPLYING THE POLISH. Far better than a messy rag. The polish even goes on more smoothly."

. . . FOR KNITTERS

"When I set my crocheting aside, I keep the THREAD from unraveling by simply slipping a safety pin through the last loop."

. . . FOR WEAKLINGS

"I just hate to struggle with those new SCREW CAPS on jars.

"I said to my husband, 'How do elderly women living alone, manage these tight new covers?' While I was struggling to open one, he went to the garage and brought back a square of sandpaper and twisted the cap right off.

"Nothing to it! Now I keep a piece of sandpaper in the cupboard and use it on all screw-type jar tops."

EASY WAYS WITH BOTTLES, BOXES AND BASKETS

From Kentucky: "I save all my PUSH-BUTTON-TYPE BOTTLES such as the kind that window cleaners, hand lotions, some starches come in. (THIS DOES NOT MEAN AEROSOL CONTAINERS, GALS!)

"I relabel the bottles and use them for scratch remover, furniture polish, spot removers, etc. They have a fine spray, and don't spill if tipped.

"I also find these bottles ideal for watering houseplants.

"I use one of these bottles for storing lemon juice in the refrigerator. I can squeeze a dozen lemons at once instead of having to squeeze one each time we want a glass of lemonade."

From New Hampshire: "Here is my trick for making ICE-COLD DRINKING WATER in a Scout or G.I.-type CANTEEN.

"Since the mouth of the canteen is too small for ice cubes, we fill the canteen about one-third full of water the night before we are going on a hike and put it into the freezer part of our refrigerator, leaving the cap off so the water can freeze. The next day we just fill the canteen (the rest of the way) with ice water and have ice-cold water for hours.

"This idea works just as well for fruit juice or other cold drinks, but don't fill the canteen too full or it won't thaw out as you need it.

"Wish I had been able to do this during my North African army days!"

From West Virginia: "When I open a NEW BOTTLE of nail polish I apply a bit of cold cream along the outside rim of the bottle. Then when I reopen the bottle the top will come off very easily—NEVER sticks."

From New Mexico: "An empty CIGAR BOX makes a fine carton for mailing small articles.

"The box is very strong, but lightweight—no heavier

244

than regular cartons. And most stores will give them to you without charge."

"I keep a pretty WICKER BASKET at the foot of the stairway, and another one by the top landing.

"Articles to be taken upstairs are put in the basket at the bottom, and items to be brought down are put in the one at the top.

"Each member of the family checks the baskets to see if there is anything to be TAKEN UP OR DOWN.

"Saves steps."

I think this idea is wonderful and can be used by all households that have an upstairs or a basement.

What's left in the baskets should be very little if you've trained each member of your family to do his bit.

ALL STEAMED UP

What to do about windows that accumulate moisture which drips during cold weather when the heat is on?

The cheapest, most satisfactory way I have found is to let a bit of moisture accumulate on your window until it becomes fogged.

Then, take three or four facial tissues and wipe the inside of the STEAMED-UP WINDOW. Wipe it until it is streaked and partially dry, and, using the SAME facial tissue, apply a dab of liquid (undiluted) household detergent, such as we wash our dishes with, and wipe the window again.

This might leave it fuzzy for a second or two, but within minutes it will be clear.

If, a week or so later, the window becomes fogged up again, just take plain, DRY facial tissues and wipe clear.

Not only do you save hours but you wash your windows at the same time!

From Missouri: "For those who want to PREVENT STEAM from accumulating in the bathroom when drawing a tub of water, run the cold water in FIRST until it reaches a depth of about an inch, then add the hot water. No steam.

THE LIGHT THAT WILL NOT FAIL

From New Jersey: "This is for fly haters . . .

"If you can't KILL THAT FLY in your kitchen at night, turn on the outside light over your back screen door, then turn off your kitchen light. The fly will go to the screen door and you can kill it.

"Works every time!"

LAY THAT SWATTER DOWN

From Georgia: "I love to open the bathroom window each morning to let in the fresh air, but, unfortunately, I do not have a screen on this window.

"I took some pretty yellow nylon net and thumbtacked it to the outside of the frame of the window.

"Now I can open my window all I want, and LAUGH AT THE FLIES on the outside!"

CORRESPONDENCE COURSE

From Nevada: "How about licking the CORNER OF THE ENVELOPE instead of licking the stamp? I just don't like glue."

It's so! You won't believe it, but try it next time you want to put a stamp on an envelope. Sure keeps the nasty tastes away. Many people have asked why they don't put cherry, chocolate, or lemon flavor in glue on stamps. Most say the flavor they taste when they lick a stamp has yet to be identified—except that it "ain't" good.

Did you know that you can UNSTICK ENVELOPES that have glued themselves shut in hot weather by freezing them a few hours in your freezer and then sliding a table knife under the flap?

The glue will still be good and you've saved all your "ruined" envelopes.

Lick your postage problem: A cut-potato surface is just moist enough to use for DAMPENING STAMPS if you haven't a sponge handy.

Just slice a small potato in two, snip off a bit of the potato on the bottom so that it will remain upright, and then slide the stamps over the top cut surface, slick as a whistle.

Works like a charm.

From South Carolina: "For avid readers: Cut a BOOK-MARK from the corner of an old envelope and slip it over the corner of a page to keep your place.

"Mark favorite recipe pages in a cookbook the same way."

EXTRA EASYS
"How do I GET THE CORK OUT of the inside of a beautiful old wine bottle? I would like to plant some ivy in it."

All you have to do is pour some straight household ammonia into the bottle, let it stand for a few days, and the cork will disintegrate. You can then pour it out. Don't be overcome by the fumes of the ammonia or put your nose over the neck of the bottle while the cork disintegrates! Always read the caution directions BEFORE using ammonia.

"I have some STERLING SILVER INDIAN BRACELETS. They are most beautiful when only the design is oxidized, yet ugly when the rest of the bracelet becomes tarnished.

"How can one clean the outside and make it shine without removing the oxidation from the design?"

Remove the bracelets from your arm. Hold them in your hand and rub (face down) briskly back and forth on any piece of wool carpet. The bracelets will shine like a brand-new half dollar.

If you do not have wool carpets, and your husband has a pair of old wool trousers, put them on your ironing board, turn down the cuff and shine the bracelets on the inside of the cuff, where it won't show. This never removes the oxidation where it should remain.

From New Mexico: "Here's a sure-fire way to PUT OUT CANDLES that does away with the usual unpleasantness of blowing them out and the risk of wax splashing on a favorite tablecloth. Or using a candle snuffer that either flattens the wick (causing future trouble) or causes that unpleasant odor and black stuff rising from the candle.

"Eliminate all this by simply letting a drop of water fall from a clean spoon onto the base of the wick. Don't touch either the wick or the wax. This is even easier to do if you use an eyedropper."

If you fasten a length of chain on the end of your CLOTHESLINE it is easier to tighten the line when it becomes slack.

Just place the next link of the chain over the hook!

"I coil my RUBBER BATH MAT (the two ends towards the center) and stand it on end in my bathtub to let it drain, instead of hanging it over the side of the tub.

"If the bath mat will not stand alone, try closing it with a colored plastic clothespin to match your decor.

"Prevents mold and mildew."

From Florida: "Here is a way to deflate an AIR MATTRESS used at a swimming pool, lake or beach: Disconnect the air plug and submerge the opposite end of the mattress in the water. The water will force all the air up to the plug. Slowly force more of the mattress under the water until it is completely submerged up to the plug.

"Be careful not to get the open plug under water!

"Now you don't have to roll, push and squeeze the air out only to find when you are finished that the mattress still has some air in it.

"And what is more useless than storing or packing a bunch of hot air?"

From Minnesota: "I always wanted an electric SHOE POLISHER so I thought of putting a lamb's-wool polishing pad (from my husband's electric hand drill) on the orange squeezer of my electric mixer. Now my shoes have a wonderful shine."

The finest POWDERED SUGAR can be made from granulated sugar by using your blender.

Just put the granulated sugar in, and cover the top. Then turn your blender on high. Result—beautiful powdered sugar which can be made as it is needed, with no more hard lumps to worry about.

Before painting a room, COVER THE DOORKNOBS with foil. It will save cleaning the spatters off later.

AUTO-EASYS

From Arizona: "Nothing is as hard on a driver as ROAD FILM on a windshield at night. It clouds everything, and in the face of oncoming lights, the white lines on the highway fade out completely.

"Neither soap, detergents nor elbow grease will remove this film. But a dash of plain grocery-store cream of tartar on a wet windshield plus a couple of swipes with a paper towel will get the glass clean."

From Ohio: "I clean the CHROME on my car bumpers with a wad of aluminum foil. I just dip it in cold water and rub away!

"It cleans the bumper like magic."

From Kentucky: "Gas station attendants sometimes let some gasoline run down the side of the car when they fill the tank. This is very difficult to remove, especially after it has dried.

"I discovered that a tablespoon of kerosene to one cup of water will remove this DRIED GASOLINE quickly."

How to Keep Your Cool

Ever think of all those little vexations we put up with? There are easy ways to deal with many of these irritations, from balky drawers to static shocks. Why not look around you and make a list of all those things that tempt you to "lose your cool." Then do something about them. It really makes life so much pleasanter.

From New Hampshire: "An alarm clock is a necessity, but the TICK-TICK-TICKING used to keep me awake at night.

"I bought a thin sponge and I keep it in my night table drawer. When I go to bed at night, I just put my alarm clock on top of that little old sponge and the sponge absorbs the ticking noise. This allows me to sleep better."

"To avoid SCRAPING the fenders of your car when driving into the garage, attach a long piece of string to a rubber ball and suspend the ball from the center of the garage doorway.

"When you drive the car into the garage, just guide it so that the ball hangs over the center of the car hood."

From California: "When you pin flowers on, push a small eraser (cut from a pencil) onto the end of the pin. The pin won't be STICKING you, and the corsage will stay firmly in place."

HIDDEN RESOURCES

Many small items we have handy can be used to solve problems they weren't really made for. So when a problem crops up and the obvious remedy isn't around, look for those "hidden resources!"

If you are temporarily without electricity, stand a FLASHLIGHT on the floor. The light will reflect on the ceiling and light the room enough to see.

Or you can place it in front of a mirror. Reflects beautifully.

From Maine: "When the windows of my car are covered with ice and snow and there is no ice scraper handy, I use a gasoline CREDIT CARD for the job.

"Works better than the scraper!"

From New Jersey: "Here is a tip for anyone who happens to break a fingernail when away from home and there's no file on hand.

"If you have a paperback MATCHBOOK, use the striking part of the matchbook to smooth your fingernail."

LET'S GET ORGANIZED

From New Jersey: "Do you hunt in vain for those elusive INSTRUCTION BOOKLETS when an appliance breaks down?

"Well, we did too, until we happened upon a simple solution:

"We now keep a nine-by-twelve-inch manila envelope in the kitchen drawer and into it go all instruction booklets and guarantees for everything from the can opener to the lawn mower, furnace, water heater, washing machine, etc.

"This has prevented many frayed nerves, and probably some service calls."

From California: "When STORING BOXES in the attic or basement, number each box with a crayon. Then number an index card and list and label what each box contains.

"Tape the cards on the back of the door to the attic or storage room. Saves you time when you go to look for some particular thing in storage."

From Virginia: "I write my marketing list on a used envelope and then carry home my TRADING STAMPS in the envelope.

"It keeps the stamps intact until I get around to pasting them in books."

From Colorado: "When you MAIL A PACKAGE and have it insured turn the receipt over and on the back write to whom the package was sent and the date. This saves many a worry."

From Kansas: "For small nail scissors, clippers and other TINY ARTICLES that get lost in your vanity drawer: Screw small cup hooks on the inside edge of the drawer and just hang them up.

"I also take a discarded leather belt and tack a strip of it to the inside of the drawer, leaving different-sized loops at irregular intervals. These little loops may be used to hold bottles of nail polish, nose drops, etc. When these are placed inside the slots they cannot possibly fall or turn over and it keeps the drawers so neat.

"I also use the above method in my kitchen drawer for small knives, and I always know where to find them."

From Connecticut: "When I was dusting my husband's RECORD COLLECTION, I noticed some of the older albums had come apart at the seams. So I hit on the idea of using colored cloth tape to put them back together. Then another idea struck me. . . . I could use various colors, depending on the contents of the album.

"Examples: Red tape for hot, swinging music, Blue tape

for blues albums. Green tape for his cool jazz. Yellow tape for light-hearted music.

"Now I keep each color together. There's a color index on the lowest record shelf, so my husband can tell at a glance what to look for."

From Alaska: "I have found many USES FOR REFLECTOR TAPE.

"Try cutting off a one-inch square of tape and putting it over the lock of your front and back door. Then cut a little slit in the tape and insert your key through it. Not only does the tape keep the moisture and dirt from getting into your lock, but it saves groping and searching for that particular spot to insert the key!

"Reflector tape is also useful along the hand rail of any stairway, especially at the bottom and the top of both rails in the basement. Anyone who has fallen down the basement steps (as I have) will know what I mean.

"Along the top and bottom steps are other good places for this tape. If you have treads, put a one-inch strip on each side at the top landing and the bottom. This will prevent many stumbles.

"I even went so far as to put bits of tape on each light switch throughout the house so that I would not soil my wife's walls when trying to find the light switch in the dark!"

NEVER AT A LOSS

Here's a hint for those who wear a watch or rings and need a good place to put them while doing dishes.

Screw a cup hook into one of your kitchen cabinets and hang your JEWELRY on this. Far safer than putting it on the kitchen window or in an apron pocket.

From Hawaii: "My BOAT KEYS used to fall out of my pocket into the water.

"Now I take a large cork, put a hole through it and fasten my key chain through the hole.

"If the keys drop from my pocket into the water, they float! No more lost keys for this boater."

From Vermont: "Here's a hint for those who must wear EYEGLASSES.

"We have our optometrist engrave the wearer's name, address and telephone number on the inside of the side bars of the frames.

"When my daughter lost her new glasses we received a phone call from the finder shortly thereafter.

"This would be especially good for those who wear prescription sunglasses and often take them off. Saves losses."

From Kentucky: "When making out CHECKS, start writing the amount as far to the left as possible on the lines provided for this purpose. This also goes for the figures.

"People should never start in the middle of the space, because the writing and the figures can easily be added to."

From Connecticut: "In my experience as a men's clothing salesman, I have seen a lot of innovations in men's suits, but I thought this one was the greatest:

"For security purposes one of my customers had a

zipper sewn across the inside pocket of his suit coat.
"He told me that when traveling abroad he keeps his
passport in this pocket. And, why wouldn't this be a wonderful idea for women who travel a lot, too? They could
have a ZIPPERED POCKET sewn inside their coats, and
keep not only their passport and ticket, but also their
traveler's checks or anything of value."

ANTICIPATE, ANTICIPATE!

"Let's say you know there's a special birthday coming
up and you want to send a card. Do you have it in plenty
of time to mail for a timely arrival? Or, suppose you lose
your car keys (it happens at least once in our lives to each
of us). Do you have an extra set concealed somewhere on
the car to save the day? If you can answer yes to these
questions, then you're the kind of person who is practiced
in keeping his or her cool. It isn't hard to do. All it takes
is planning ahead.

And let's consider those accidents that can be prevented
by a little advance planning. NEVER throw away MEDICINE
AND PILL BOTTLES unless you first empty the contents
down the toilet! Then flush it immediately!

Never put half-full bottles of anything in your garbage
either. Lots of people do this, especially when they clean
out their medicine cabinets.

Little children just love to go through neighbors' trash
cans and play with bottles. Pets often get into garbage
cans, too. They don't know any better either.

So, take the time to empty all medicine containers. You
might save a life.

"I ripped out just enough stitching at the top of the
label that is sewn into my coat to insert a DIME.

"Should I lose my purse or find myself without change, I can at least make a phone call."

"I carry two small PLASTIC BAGS and a couple of rubber bands in my purse and I find them very useful when caught in a rainstorm.

"I pull one bag over each shoe and fasten them with the rubber bands. The plastic covers protect the shoes and ankles. No ruined shoes or wet feet."

"When I go on a trip or any place where simple FIRST-AID treatment might be needed, I pack the following into an empty metal adhesive-bandage container.

"Book of matches, needle, tweezers, several different sizes of plastic bandage strips, empty pill bottle of alcohol, empty pill bottle of peroxide, and a little cotton.

"Yes, this will all fit inside the little box, approximately 3″ x 4″ x 1½″. It is small, compact, and with its bright enamel finish, can be easily spotted when it's needed."

An empty match cover makes a neat little REPAIR KIT to carry in your purse.

After all the matches are used, stick a few pins and a needle in the edge where the matches have been torn out, wind various colored thread around the cover, fold the cover and put in your purse.

Lots of people paint the covers or use plastic-back adhesives to cover the outside, and give them to friends. Real perky idea, I'd say.

"An empty waxed milk carton makes an excellent FLARE in case of car trouble. It will burn for as long as 15 minutes.

"It's good to carry a few empty ones in the back of your car for emergencies."

AID TO THE ABSENTMINDED

From Michigan: "Have you ever arrived home, opened your purse, and discovered you didn't have a KEY to open the door?

"I have eliminated this nuisance by burying a small jar behind a large plant near the back door and keeping an EXTRA DOOR KEY in it. I bury the jar just deep enough to be covered by only a small amount of dirt."

We have purposely not used your location as we would hate to be responsible for someone digging up your plants!

From Kansas: "I always prepare my HUSBAND'S LUNCH the night before and put it in the refrigerator.

"Many times he'd forget to take it.

"I now put his car keys in the refrigerator with his lunch!"

From Massachusetts: "For years I have been putting notes in my husband's pocket, as a reminder to do a certain errand for me.

"But most of the time he'd forget to look in his pocket!

"Finally, he came up with an idea that really works.

"I put the note inside the clear cellophane wrap over his CIGARETTE PACK!

"No chance of his missing it there!"

MIRROR, MIRROR, TELLS IT ALL

Here's how a lady in New York helps keep the path of true love smooth.

"Have a petty complaint that must be aired? For instance, 'who left the bottle of shampoo on the side of the tub where the little ones could get it and pour it out (Oh, the poor budget), or worse yet, break it and cut themselves?'

"A little MIRROR note to the offender will get your point across.

"Anyway, it beats nagging and seems to get the job done."

FOR THAT LEISURELY LADY LOOK

The theme of the crowning glory story is neatness. And a neat HAIRDO doesn't happen by accident. Here's a hint for those ladies and teenage girls who set their hair. Let me tell you the proper way to remove those rollers—particularly if your hair is long.

Unroll them the OPPOSITE way they were rolled up.

Starting at the neckline, unfasten each roller gently, and pull it DOWN toward the shoulder. This will keep the hair from tangling and pulling.

Go around the head from one side to the other, and

as each roller is loosened, pull it DOWN again—OVER the last curl you unrolled.

When you get to the top of the head, undo the one toward the back first—again pulling each one toward the back and down again.

When you first start combing or brushing the curls, do it the same way you removed the rollers—starting at the neck and proceeding upward.

This will make the hair easier to comb or brush out, and will help hold the set in place in case one or more curls are still slightly damp.

From Pennsylvania: "To keep HAIR in place at night:

"Simply take a clean, old nylon stocking and cut it all the way down the center back, including the foot part.

"At night, wrap this around your hair, and just crisscross the nylon on the top front of your hair (no need to tie or pin it in place), then put a hair net over it.

"I keep my hair style in place all week this way."

From California: "Are you tired of getting your HAIR wet, especially in the back, every time you take a shower? Here's a solution.

"Fold a wash cloth or fingertip towel and place it IN-SIDE your shower cap at the neck line. The towel or cloth might get wet, but your hair stays dry."

From Ohio: "Tie on a plastic, accordion-pleated rain bonnet the next time you start to don a tight dress or sweater. The material slides easily over the slick plastic, and the ties under the chin keep the bonnet from slipping.

"Your HAIRDO will remain intact.

"One of these rain bonnets in your purse will also help the next time you are out shopping for dresses."

From Michigan: "I use the middle of my emery boards for sharpening the points of my EYEBROW pencils. It gives them as sharp and fine a point as you could possibly want."

From Connecticut: "For those of you who like to wear your BLOUSES out, but find that the bottom of the blouse is so large it makes you look pounds heavier, here's the solution:

"Lay the blouse wrong side out on the ironing board, and in the back, down near the hem, make two pleats. Join the pleats together with a piece of iron-on tape, iron it on, and presto! The blouse takes on a new look and you look pounds smaller."

"After huffing over GIRDLES for years, I've figured out an easier way to put one on.

"Now, I put on my stockings FIRST. This eliminates that armorplated bending to meet the toes. Then I put on the girdle, pulling it up just far enough to fasten the garters to the stockings. Then the girdle can be pulled on up around the hips, hooked, and zipped."

"I wear a clean old pair of cotton gloves while making beds, shaking rugs, etc.

"Sure saves a lot of FINGERNAILS."

From Rhode Island: "As soon as I have finished shampooing my hair, and while it is drying, I MANICURE my nails while I am sitting under the drier. Two things accomplished in the time it takes for one."

"Put a facial tissue (folded in half) in each SHOE before putting it on, especially if you are not wearing stockings.

"This not only absorbs the perspiration but gives longer life to shoes, since perspiration rots leather.

"Being a podiatrist, I recommend this to all my patients, especially the men who wear black socks.

"I tell the gentlemen to open two facial tissues for each foot and place one on top of the other, set their feet on them, wrap the tissues around their feet, and then pull on their black socks.

"My patients now say that they can stand on their feet longer each day without having their feet become tired. It has helped many."

From Kansas: "For those of you who have a shower and not a bathtub and would like to have the feeling of relaxing in a tub of water, the next best thing to do is don a terry cloth or chenille robe and just stand under your shower! (A bath towel will also do it if you have no robe of this sort.)

"When the flow of water hits your robe or towel it will cause a relaxing HOME STEAM BATH. Very refreshing."

Folks, you all should try this. It's absolutely amazing.

I found it good to use two towels (one wrapped around the waist and the other across the shoulders) if you have no robe.

From Washington: "A handy gadget to carry in your handbag to PICK UP LINT and brush cloth shoes is a plastic foam hair roller.

"It's compact, washable, flexible and does the job in a jiffy."

MAKE TIME FOR FUN

During the holidays, when many people do a lot of entertaining, I wonder if they realize how much easier— and less expensive—it is to give small PARTIES on two consecutive nights, rather than to have them a couple of weeks apart?

Since you have given the house a good cleaning before the first party, all you have to do is put it back in order.

If you have bought fresh cut flowers, they will still be fine for the second night—THERE's a saving of 100%!

You probably bought a variety of salad greens, and only used part of each kind—plus parsley (and who ever uses a whole bunch at one time?).

If you are serving a casserole, make twice as much as you need for the first party, and save half of it for the second.

Or, if you're planning on having a big turkey or ham dinner, get large ones and have a cold, buffet dinner the second night.

Sure, you may be tired after giving two parties in a row, but I'll bet you'll thank yourself for trying it this way when you realize how much time, energy (less cleaning, and just ONE trip to the grocery store), and money you saved.

From Oklahoma: "I just hate to waste LOVELY DAYS doing chores, so I resolved that when it's raining or my child is sick and I can't go anywhere I do things like cleaning closets or windows and other jobs that have accumulated.

"Then, on nice days, I can go out and enjoy the day with an easy conscience."

THE HELOISE MAD BOX

Why not make yourself a little Heloise MAD BOX?

It works wonders when something has got your dander up.

We all get so mad and full of frustrations that some days we think we are going to explode. Sometimes the things that cause us to explode one day won't even bother us the next day. They seem so simple and we wonder why in this wide wide world we got mad and said things we are sorry for. And once it's said, it can't be taken back!

Here's what I do:

When I get mad, I go to my typewriter (if you haven't one, use pencil and paper) and put down all the little irritating things.

THEN HIDE YOUR LETTERS!

Write them to your husband and children (each one separately) but keep them hidden in your secret Mad Box and NEVER deliver them.

DON'T look at those letters for at least four days!!! Then take some more paper and a pencil, go into your bathroom or bedroom, lock the door and rewrite the letter or letters.

See how much shorter it is?

And you can bet that nine times out of ten, you'll soon tear them all up.

My Mad Box idea is in two parts and the second part is my ABOUT-TO-WORRY BOX.

List all your about-to-worries on a piece of paper. This includes bills, overexpenditures, payments due, cleaning to be done, kitchen needing new paint, noisy muffler on the car, water heater needing replacing, worn rug, etc., etc. (Oh, I could write forever about all the troubles you and I have had.)

You can share this list with your husband, but not for a few months!

So start your own personal Mad Box. I think you will find it invaluable. You can rework it every few days and cross off your worries as they are solved—watch that list dwindle. Psychiatrists with whom I have talked agree with me that nine-tenths of the things we worry about never come to pass.

I PROMISE that the day will come when you will find that most of your troubles will be answered—by you yourself, which is the best way in the world.

Try my method. It works!

Look at the good things that happened today! And tomorrow is yet to come!

Index

For Your Notes